This coloring book belongs to:

____

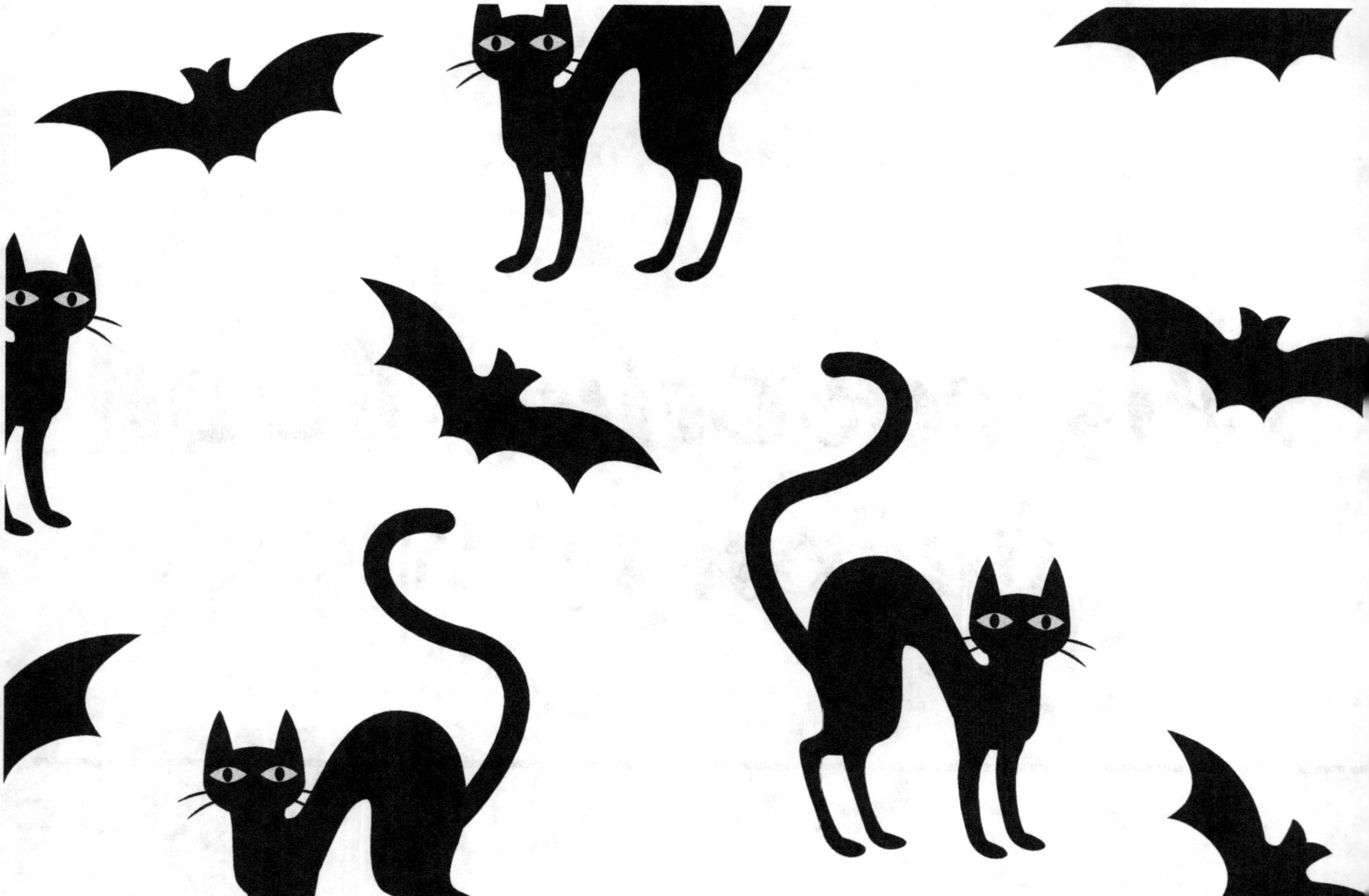

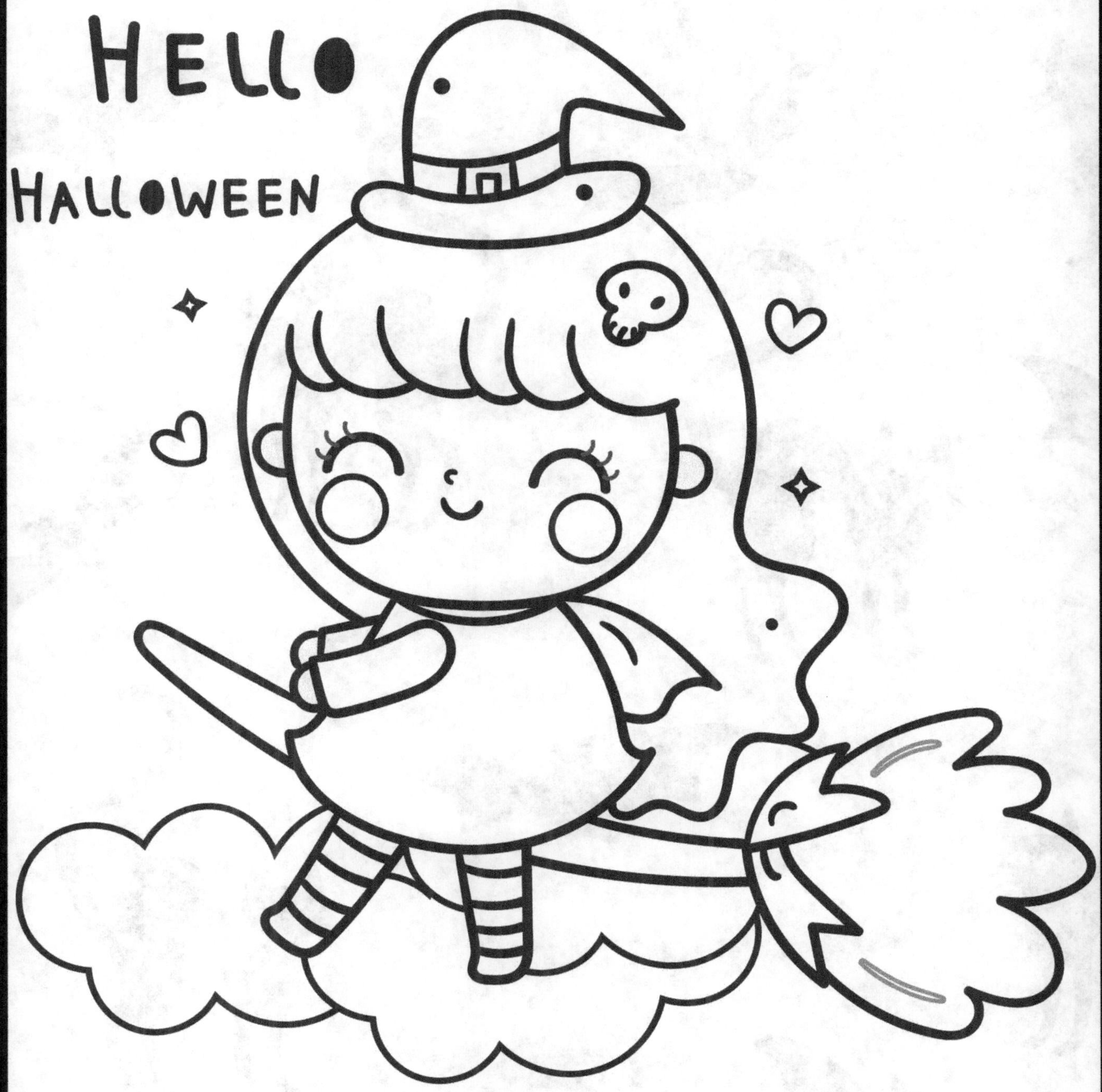
HELLO
HALLOWEEN

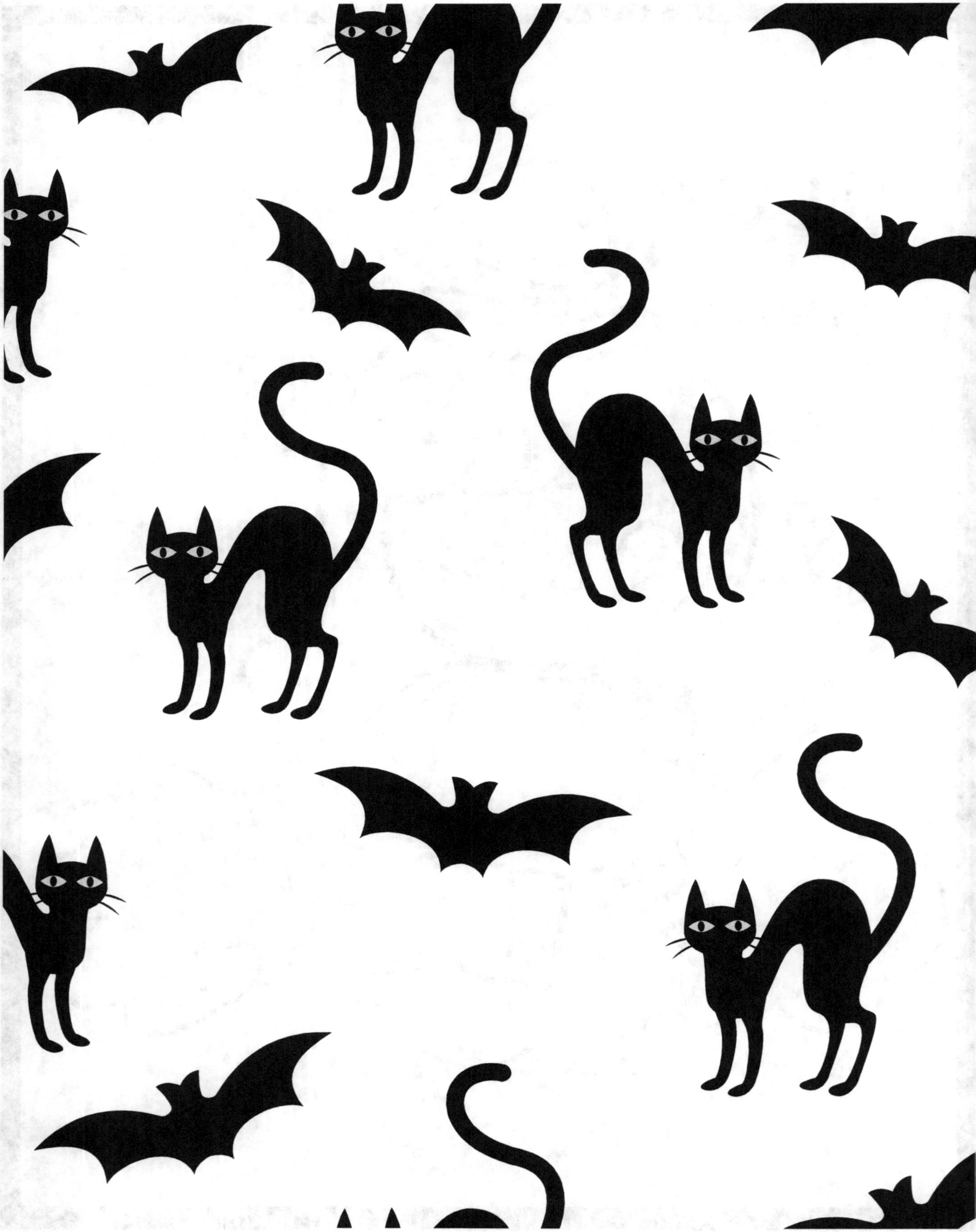

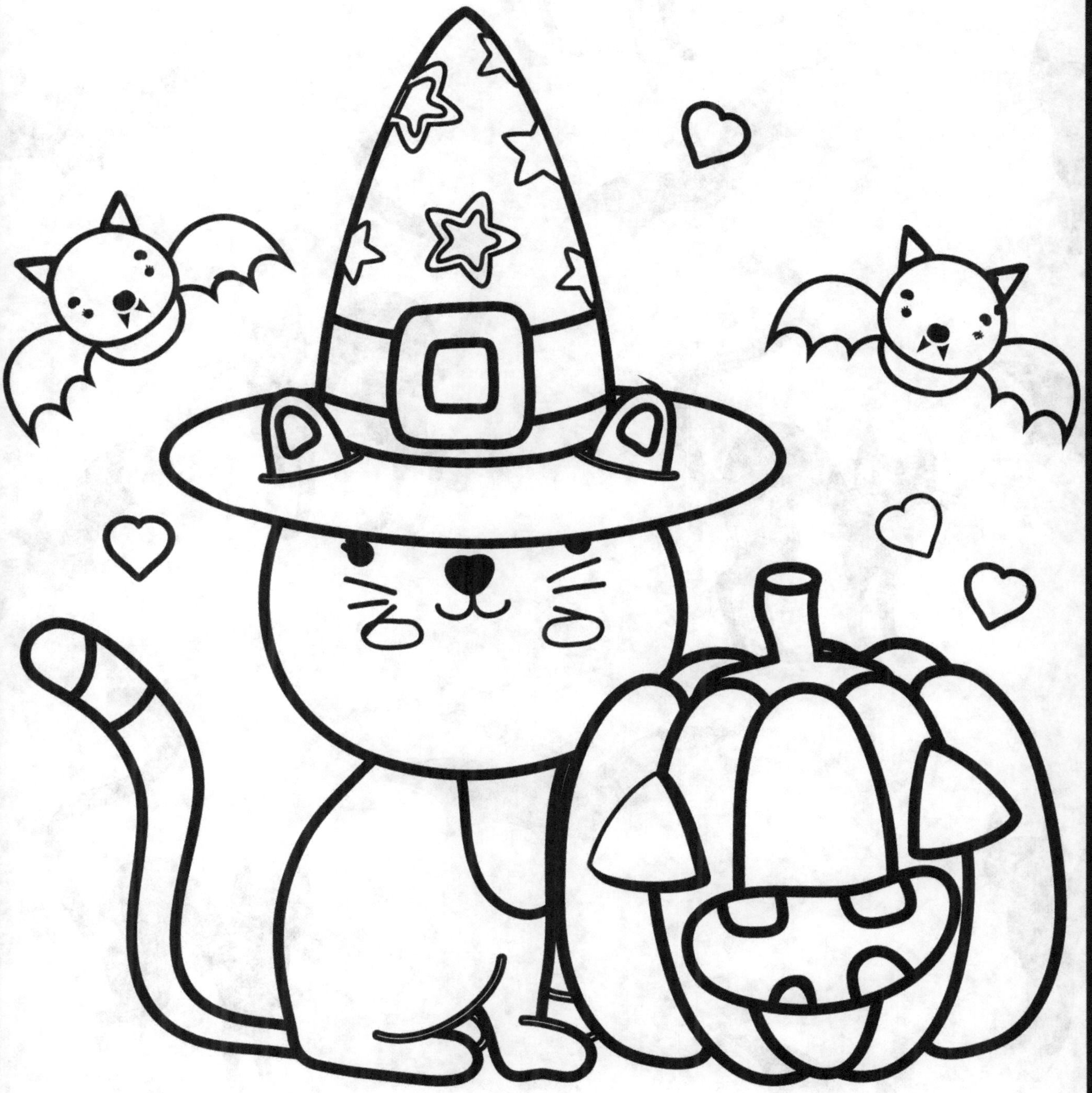

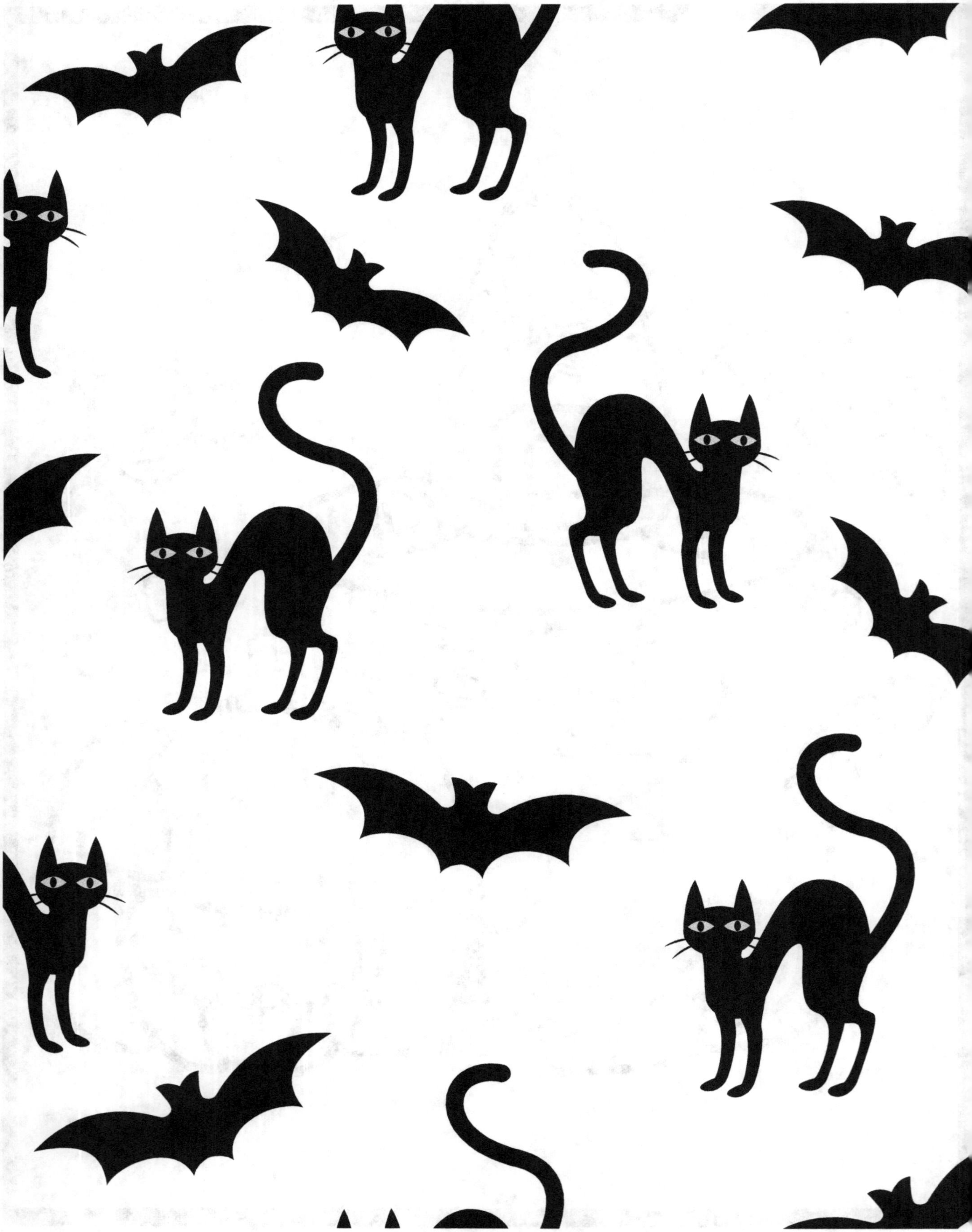

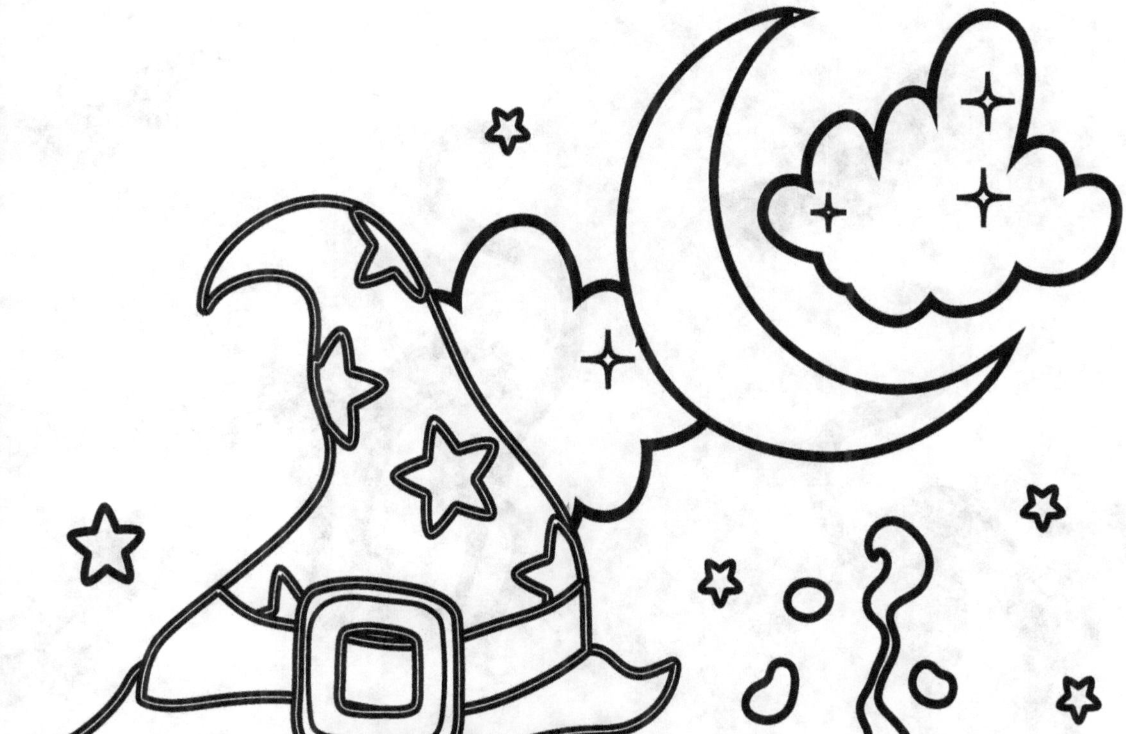

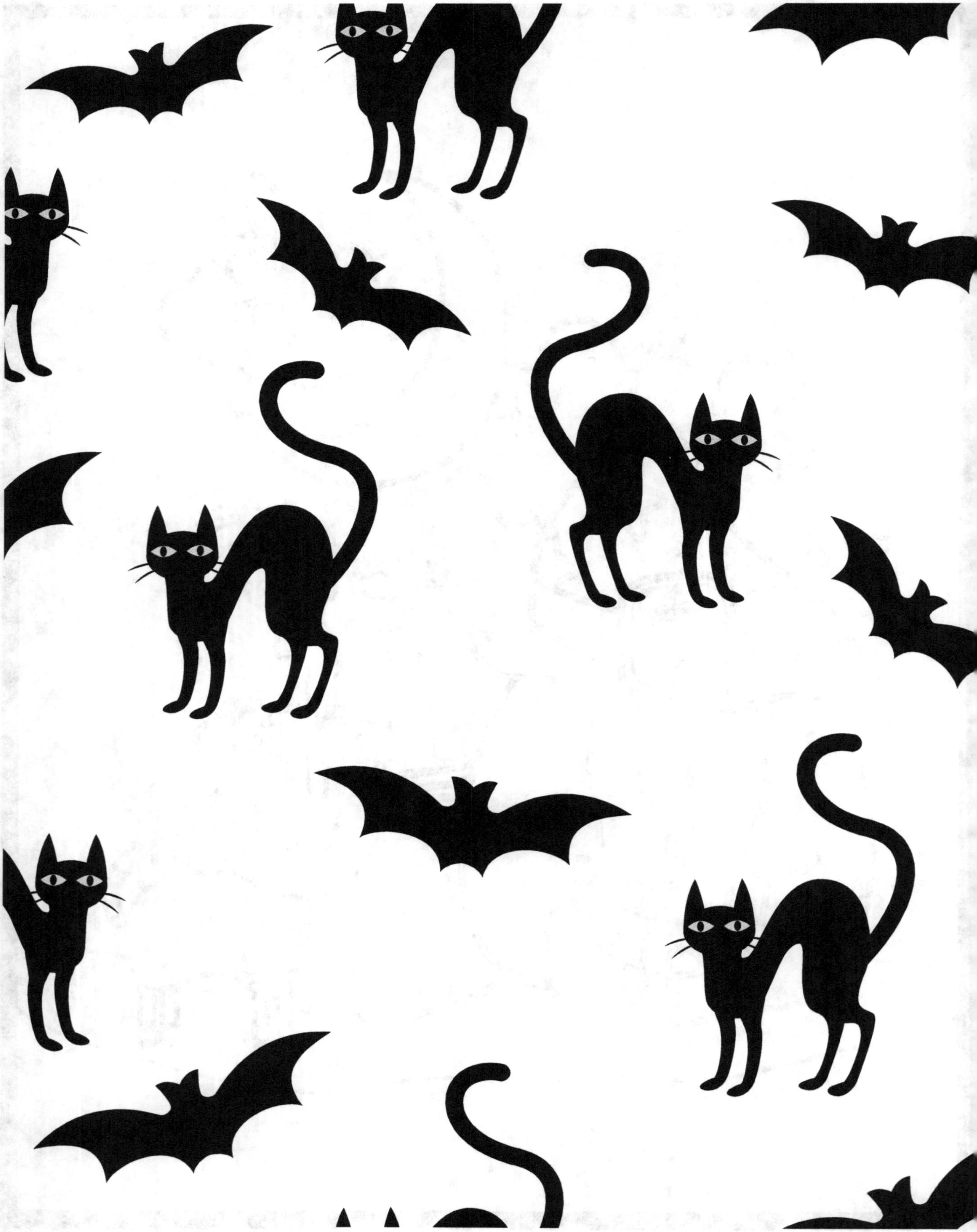

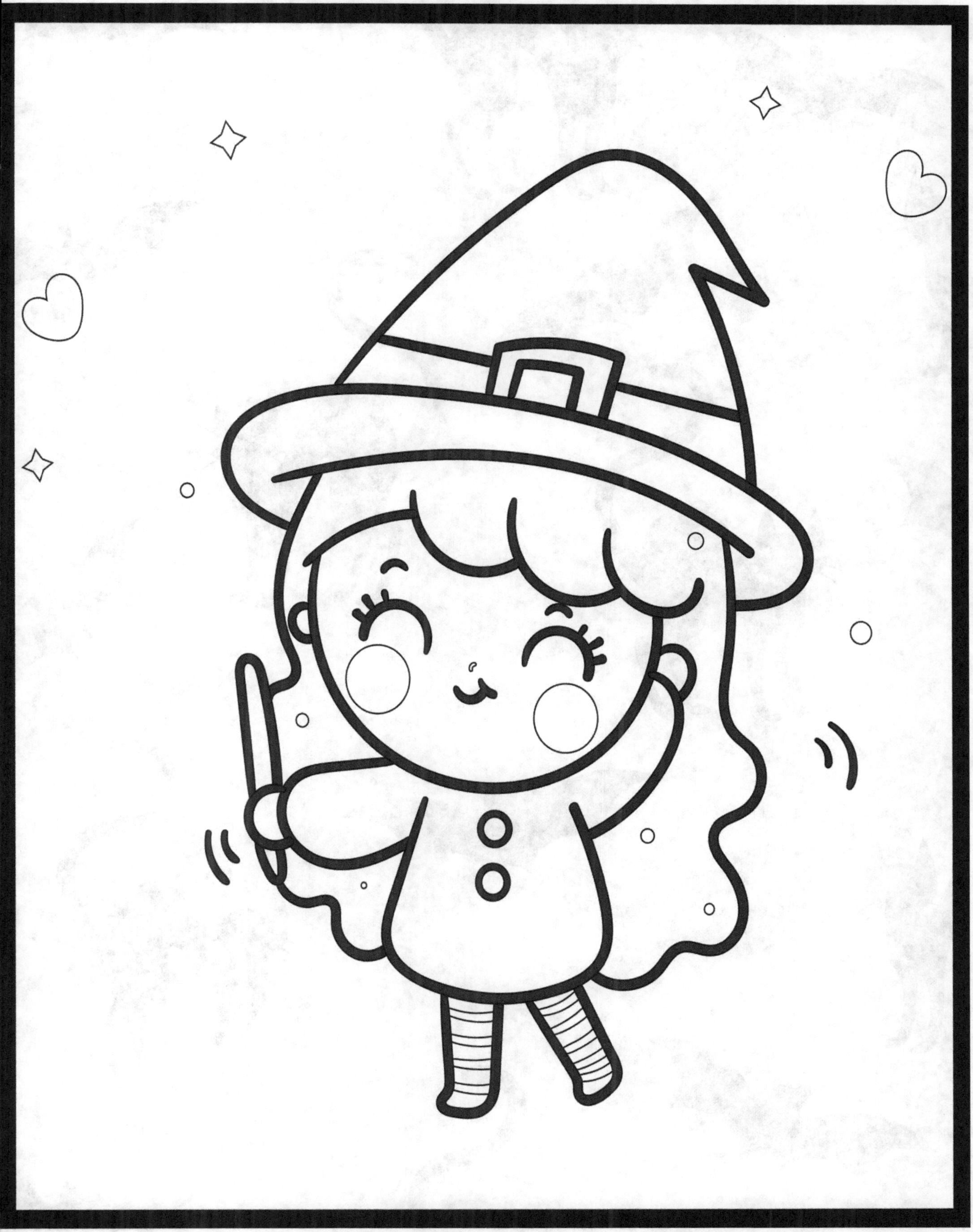

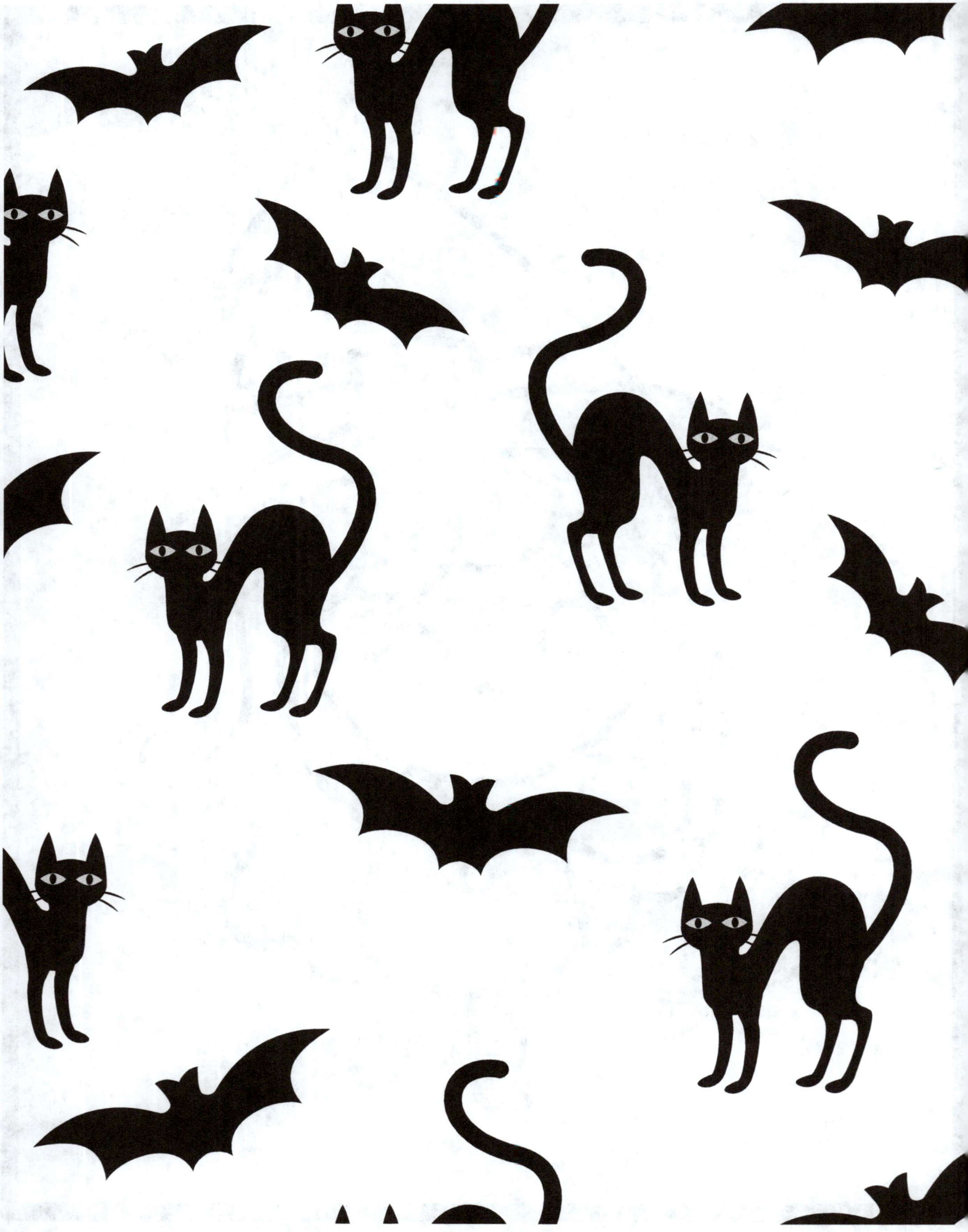

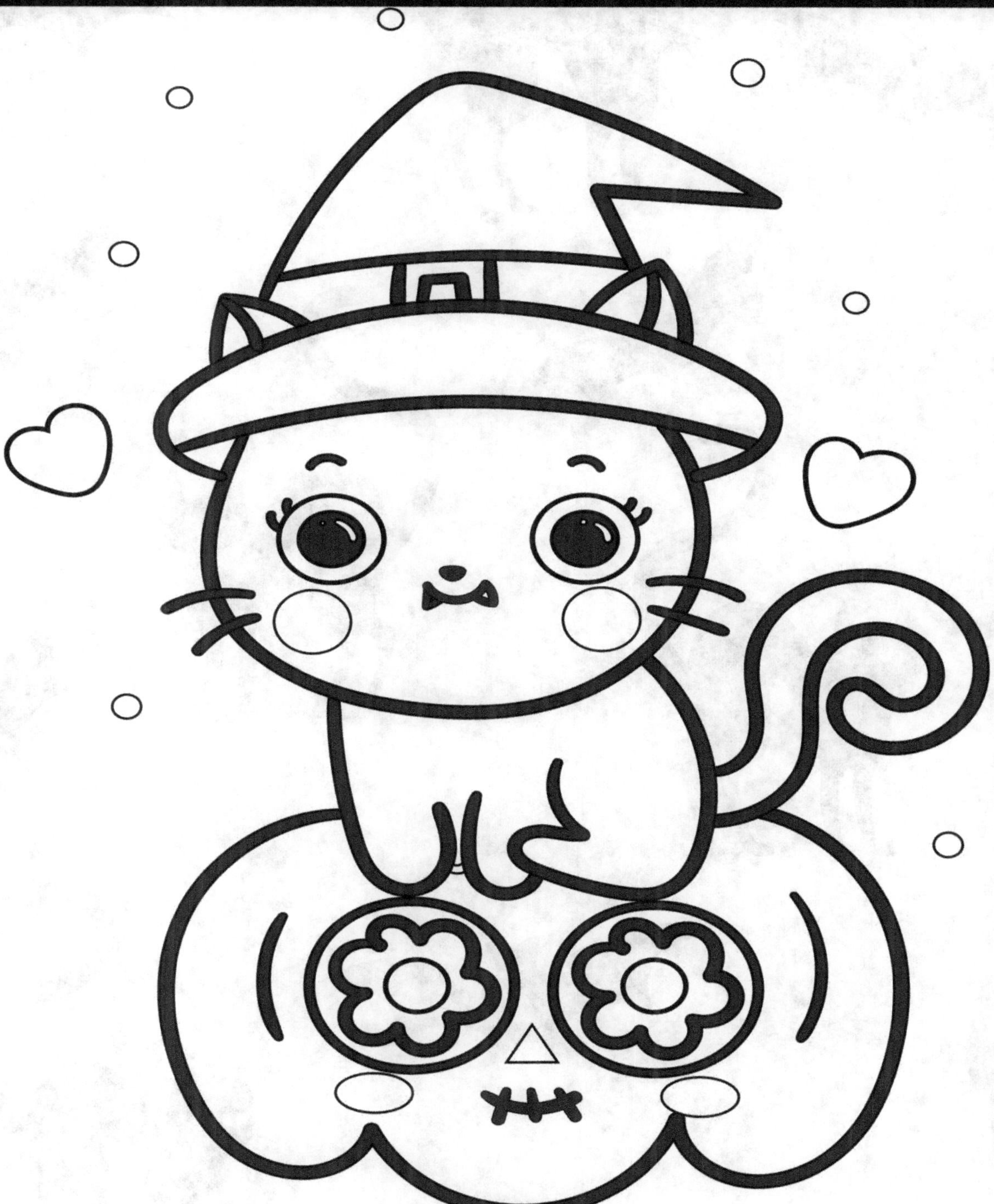

HAPPY
HALLOWEEN

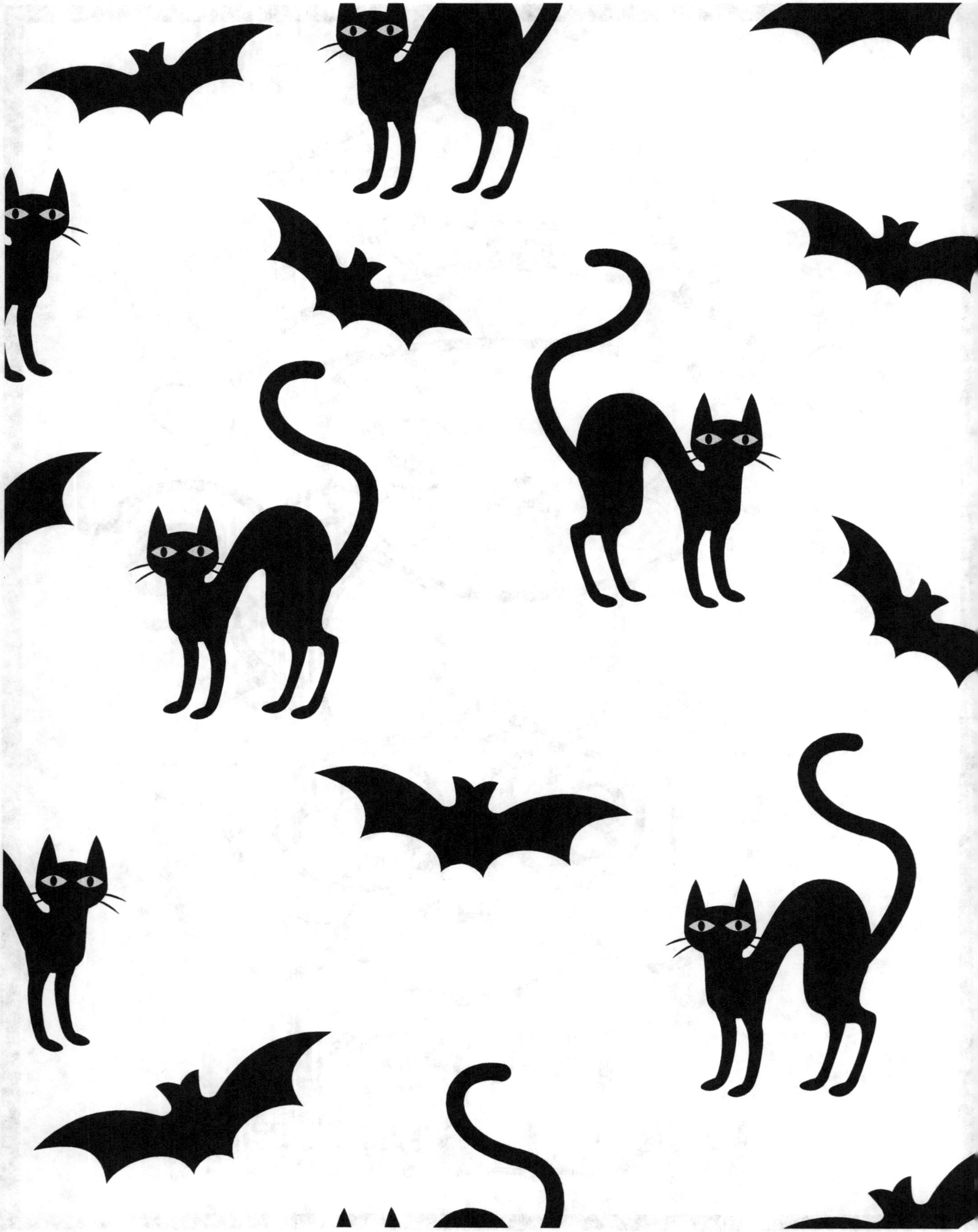

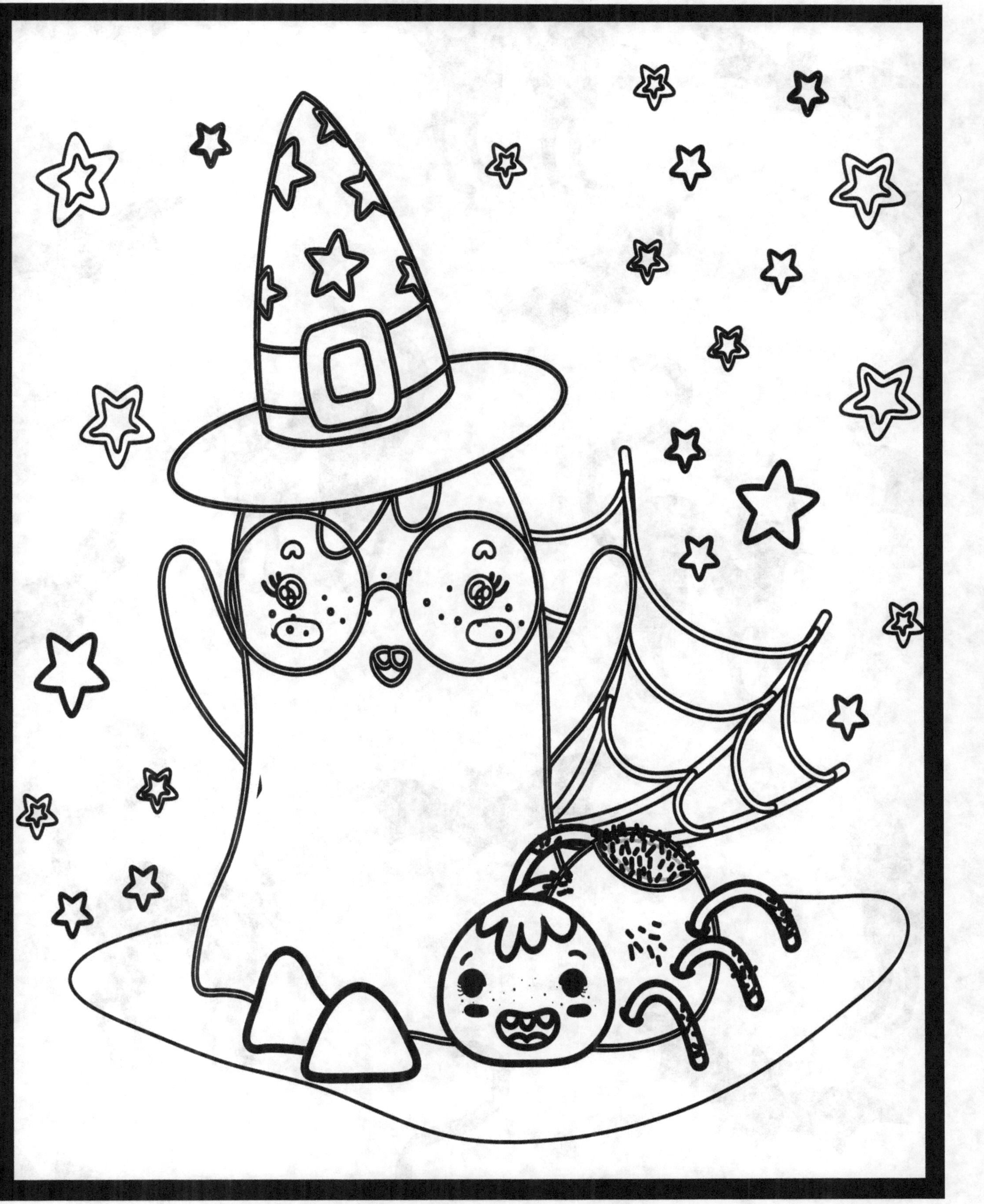

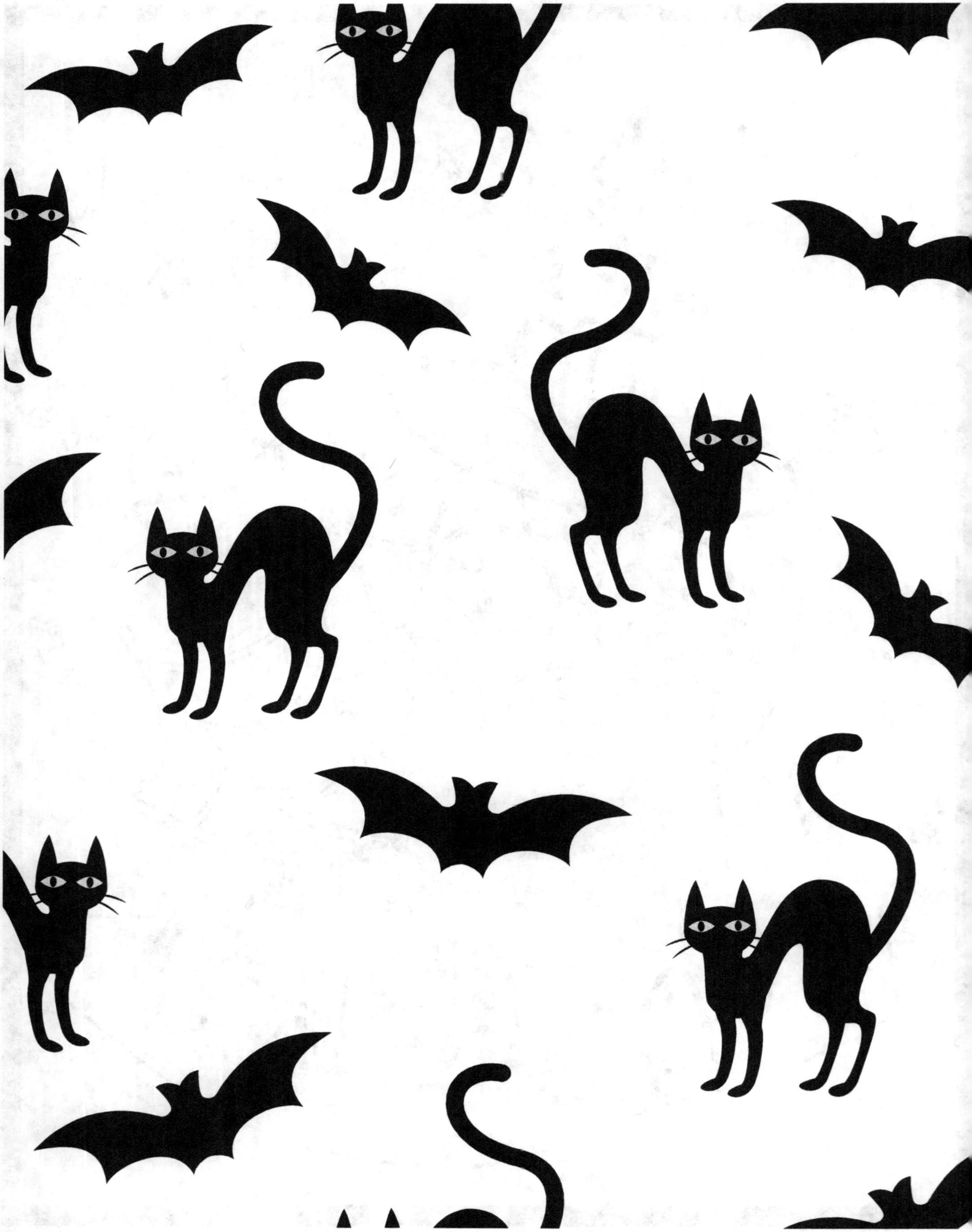

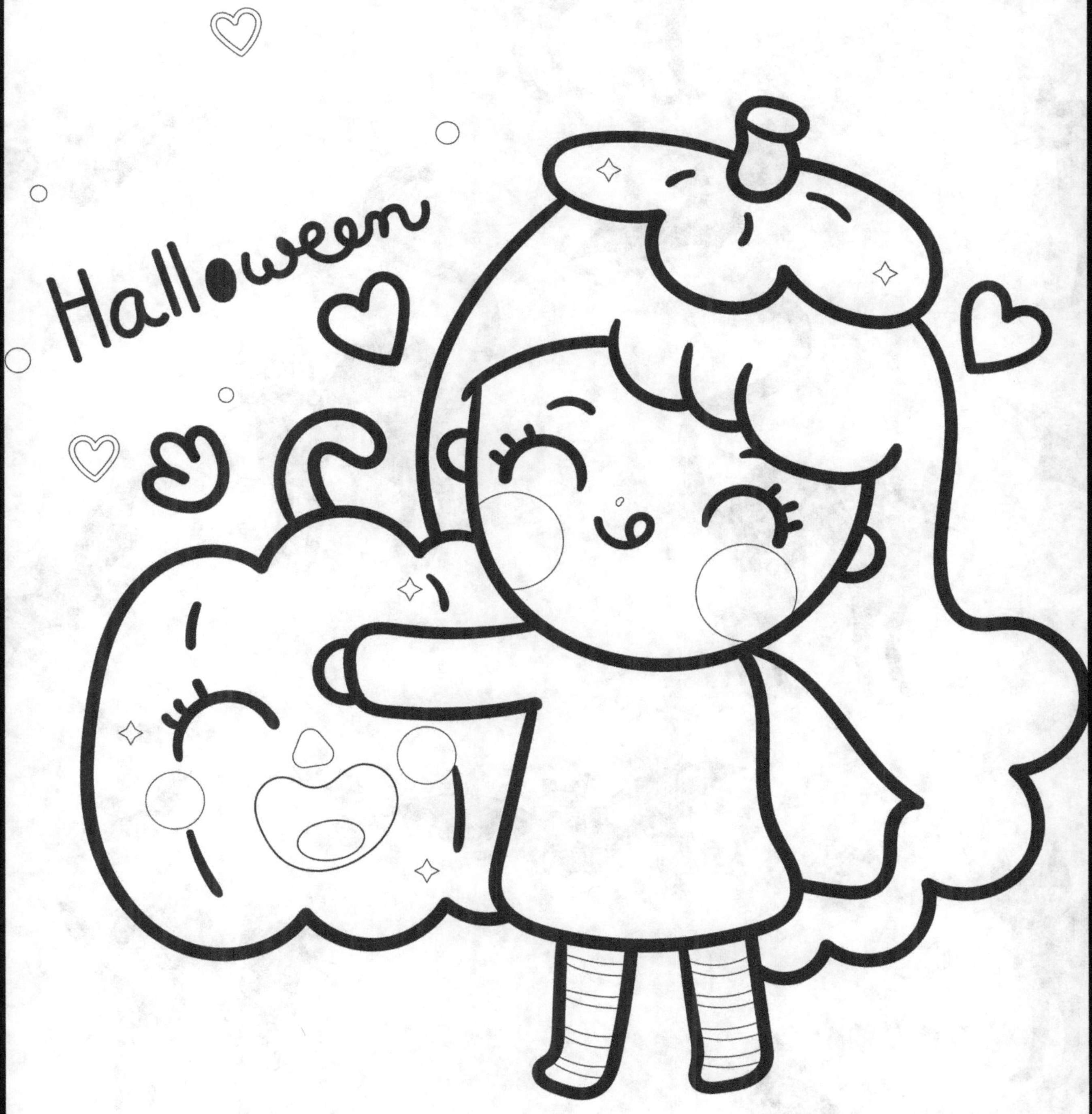
Halloween

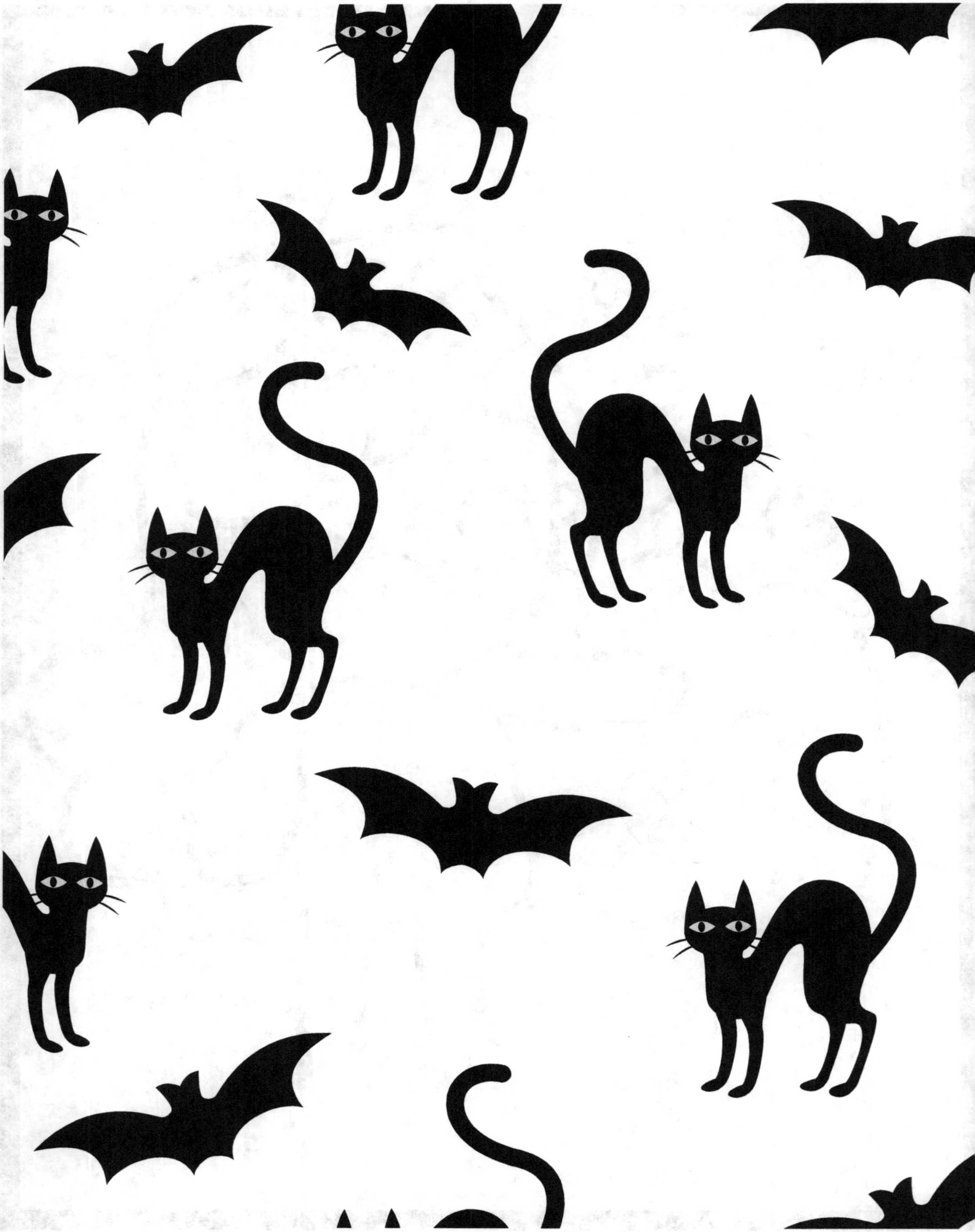

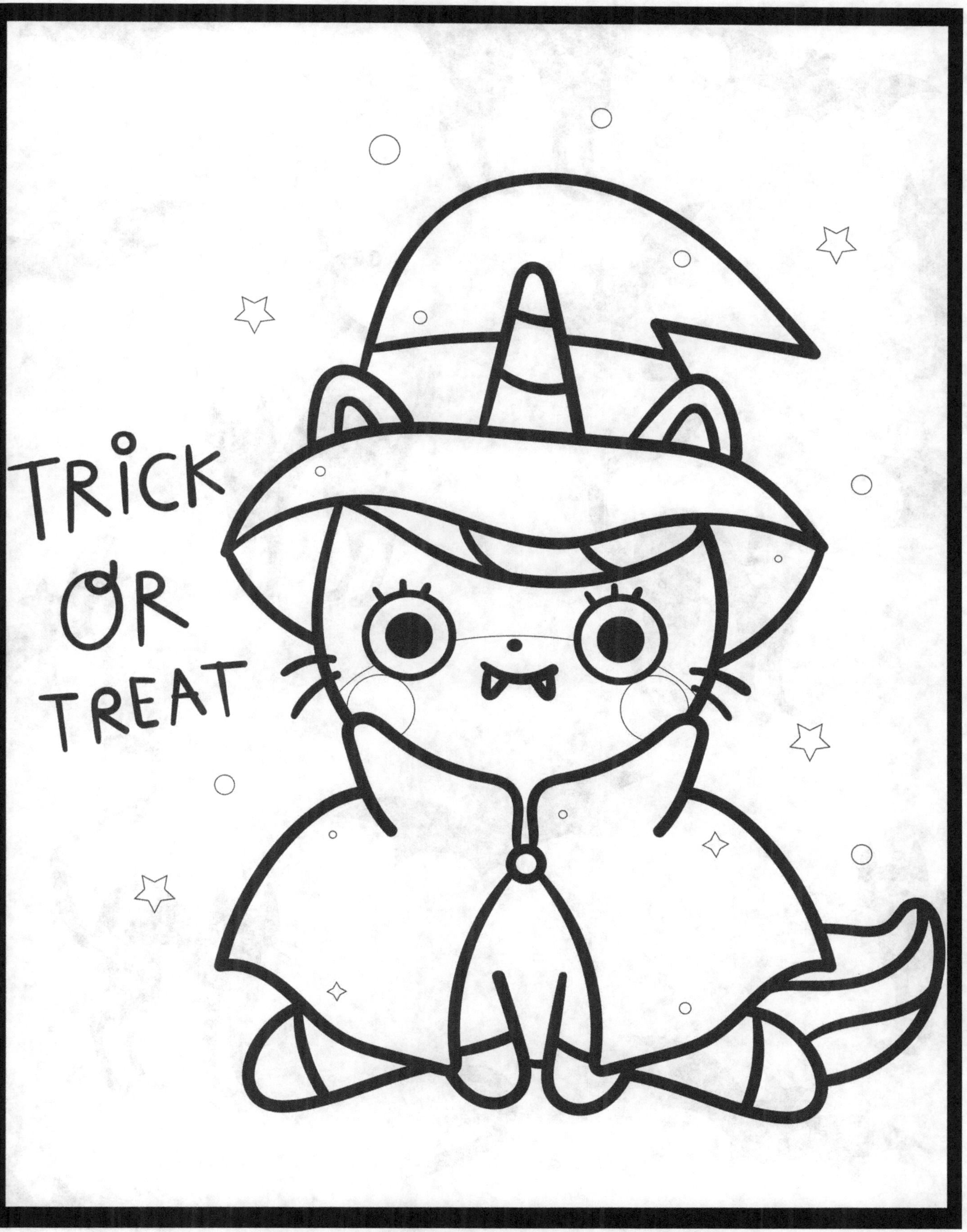
TRICK
OR
TREAT

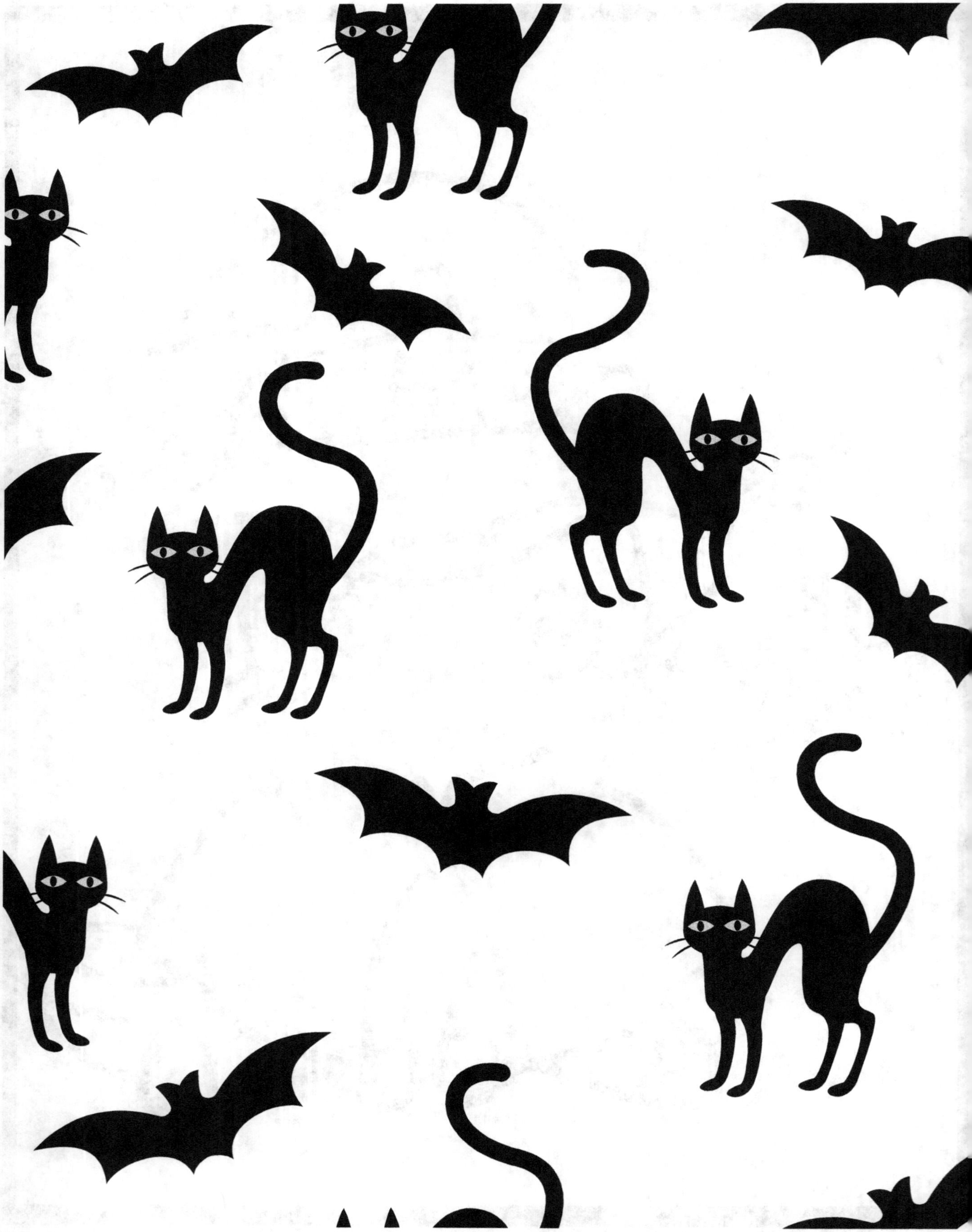

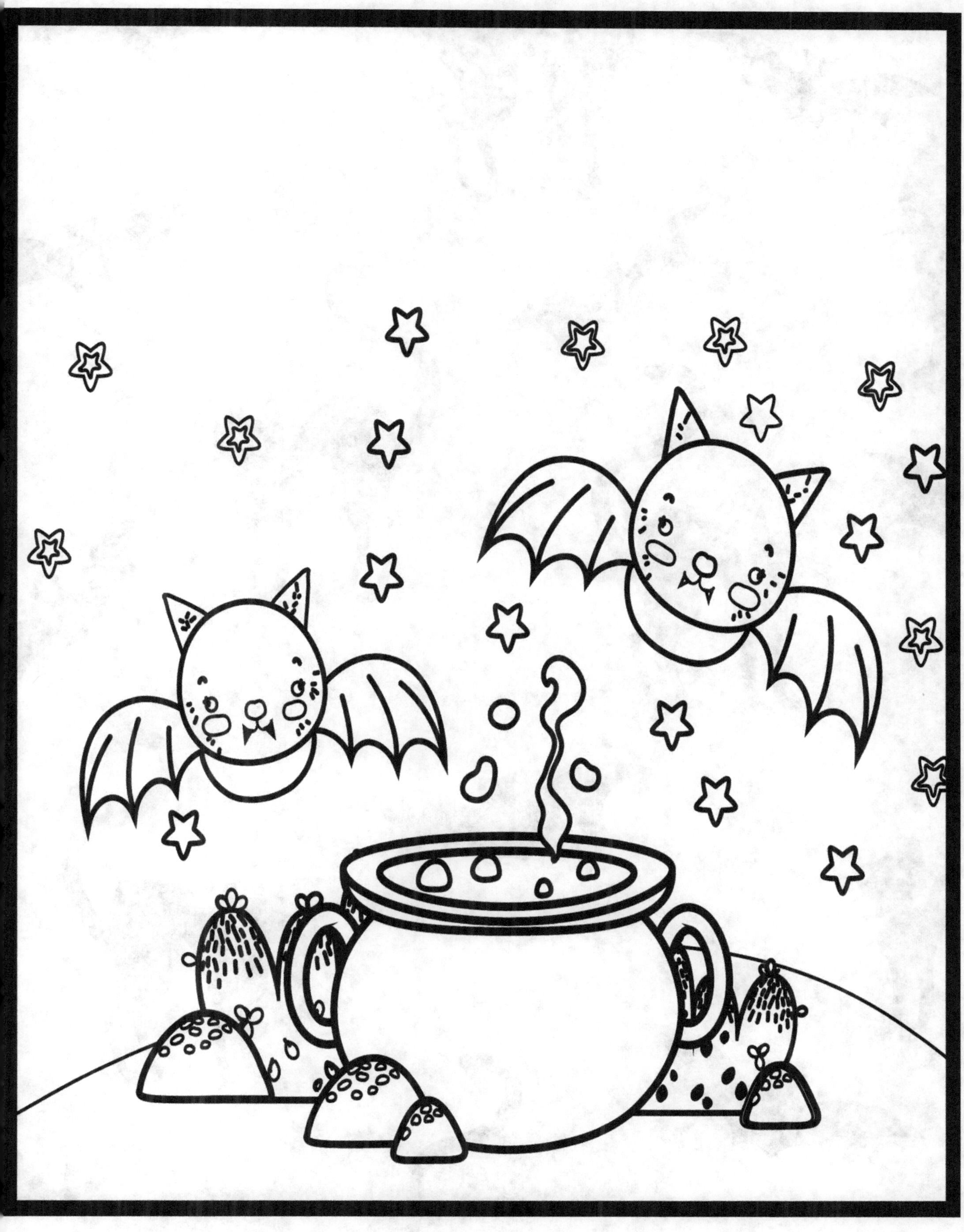

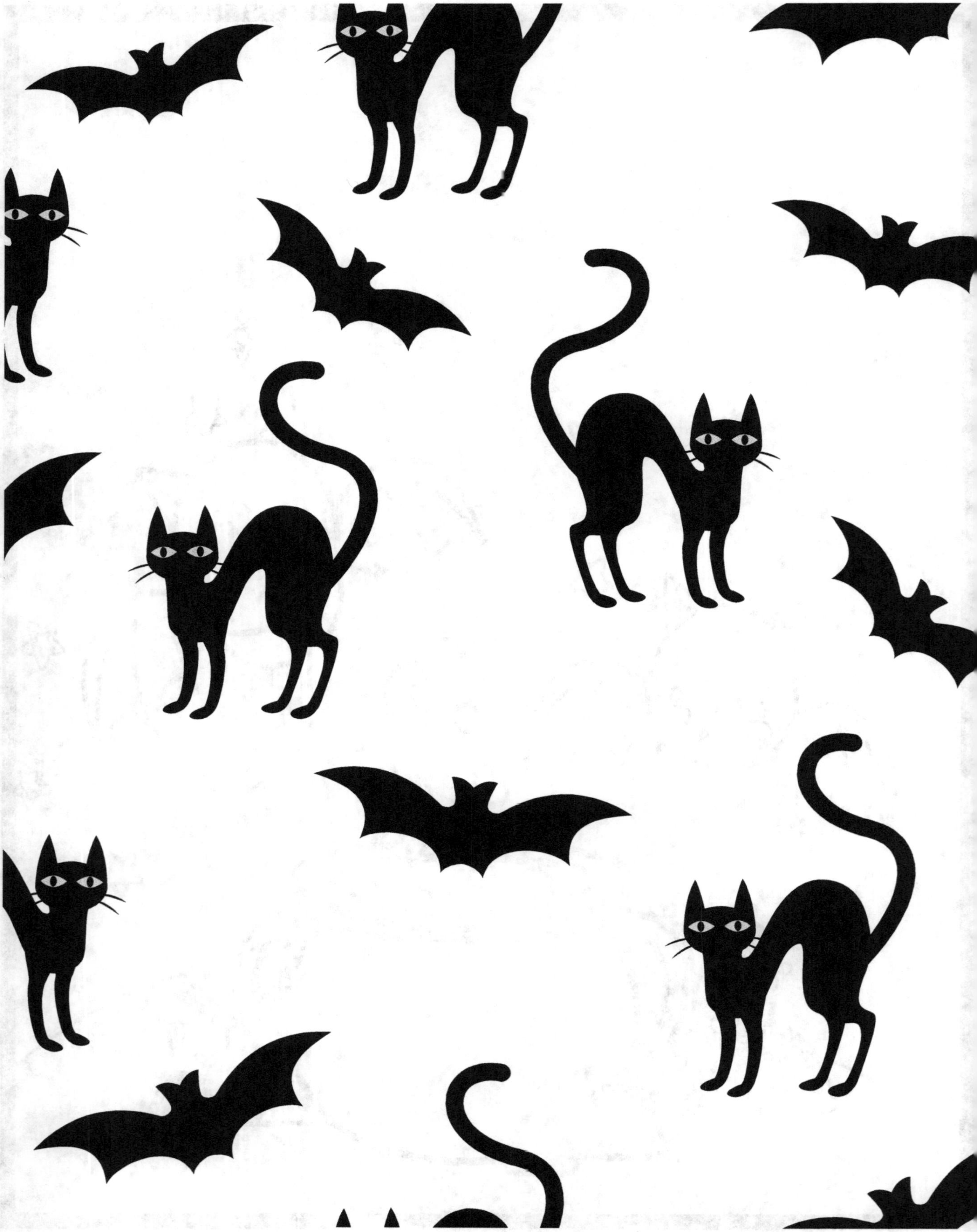

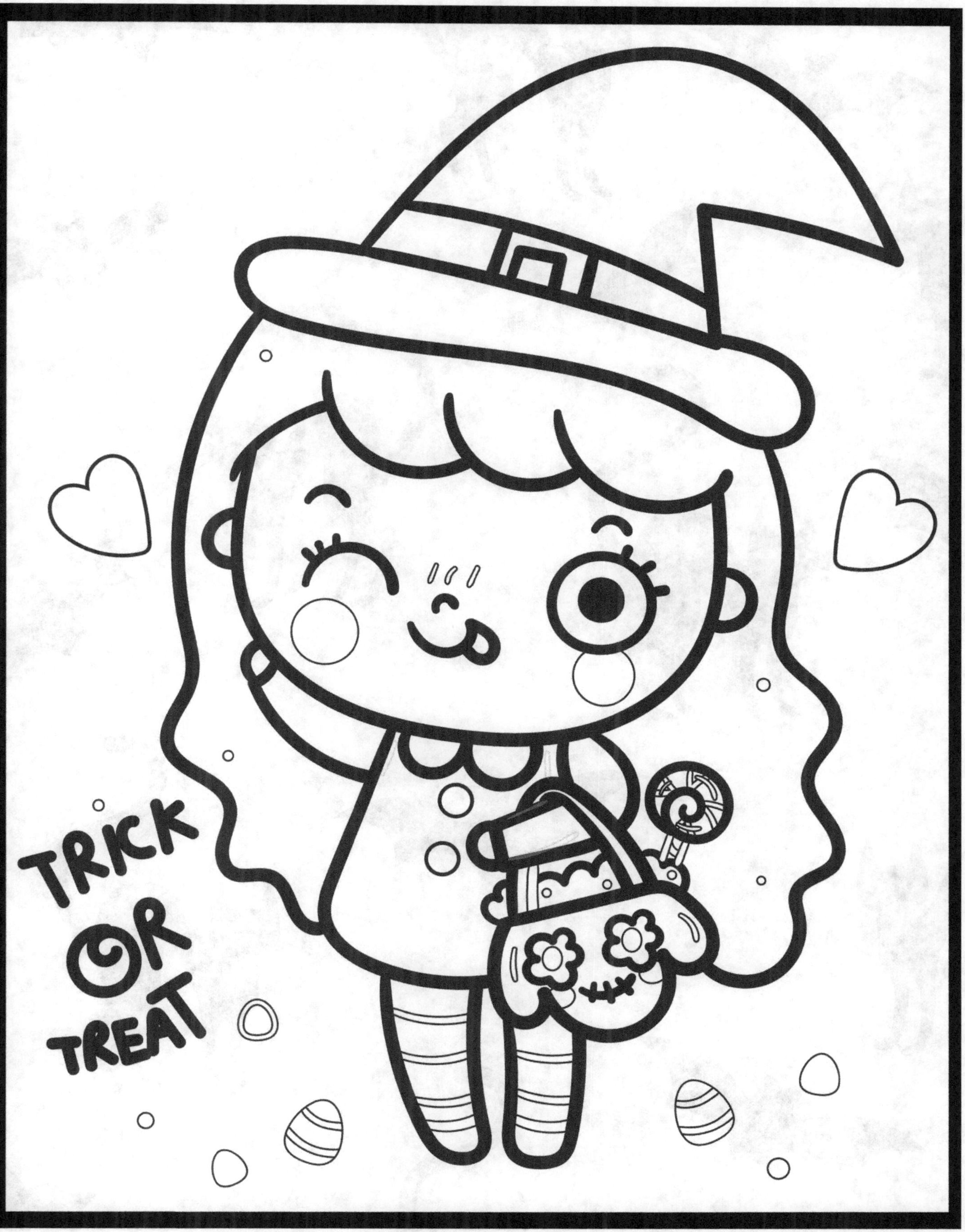
TRICK
OR
TREAT

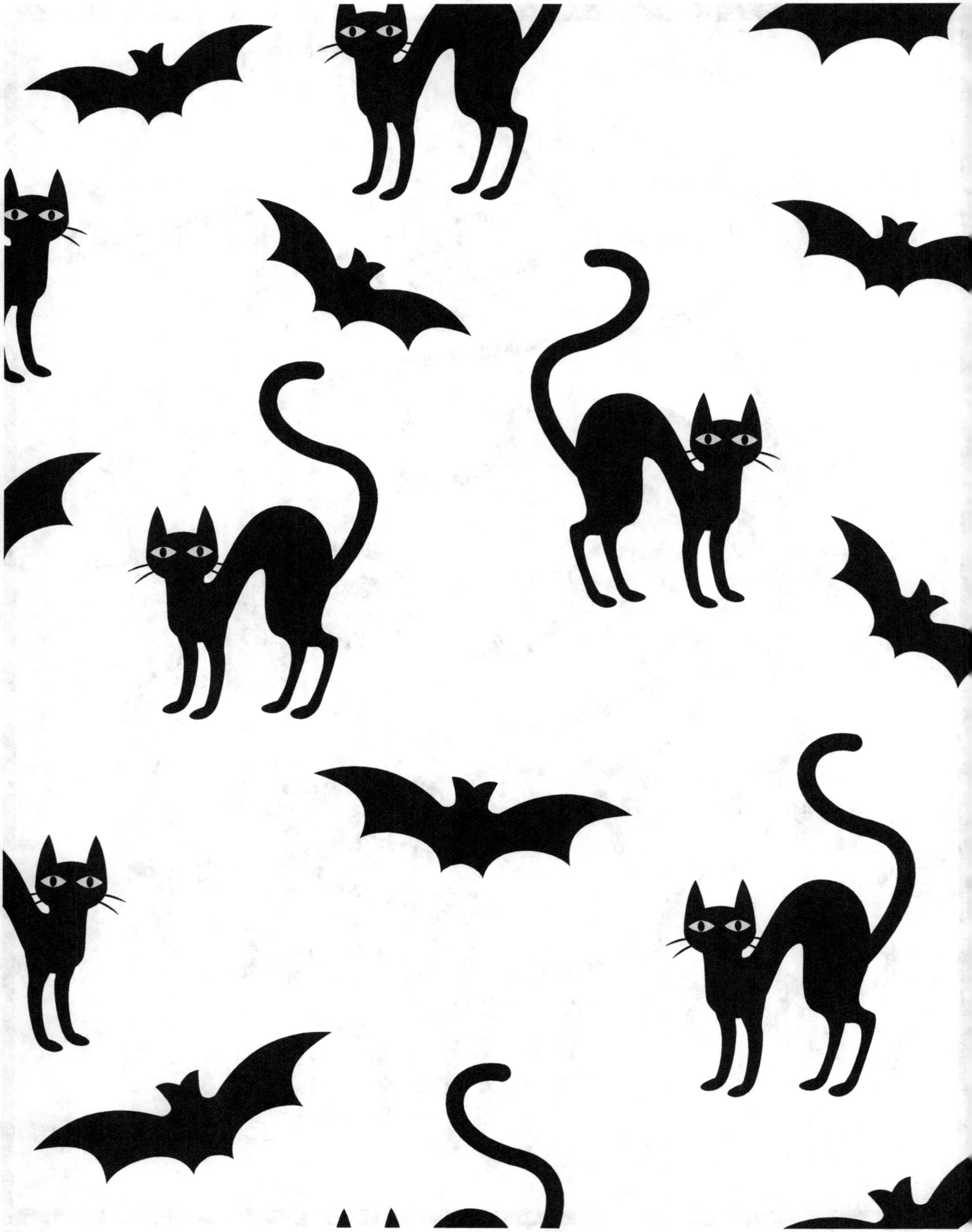

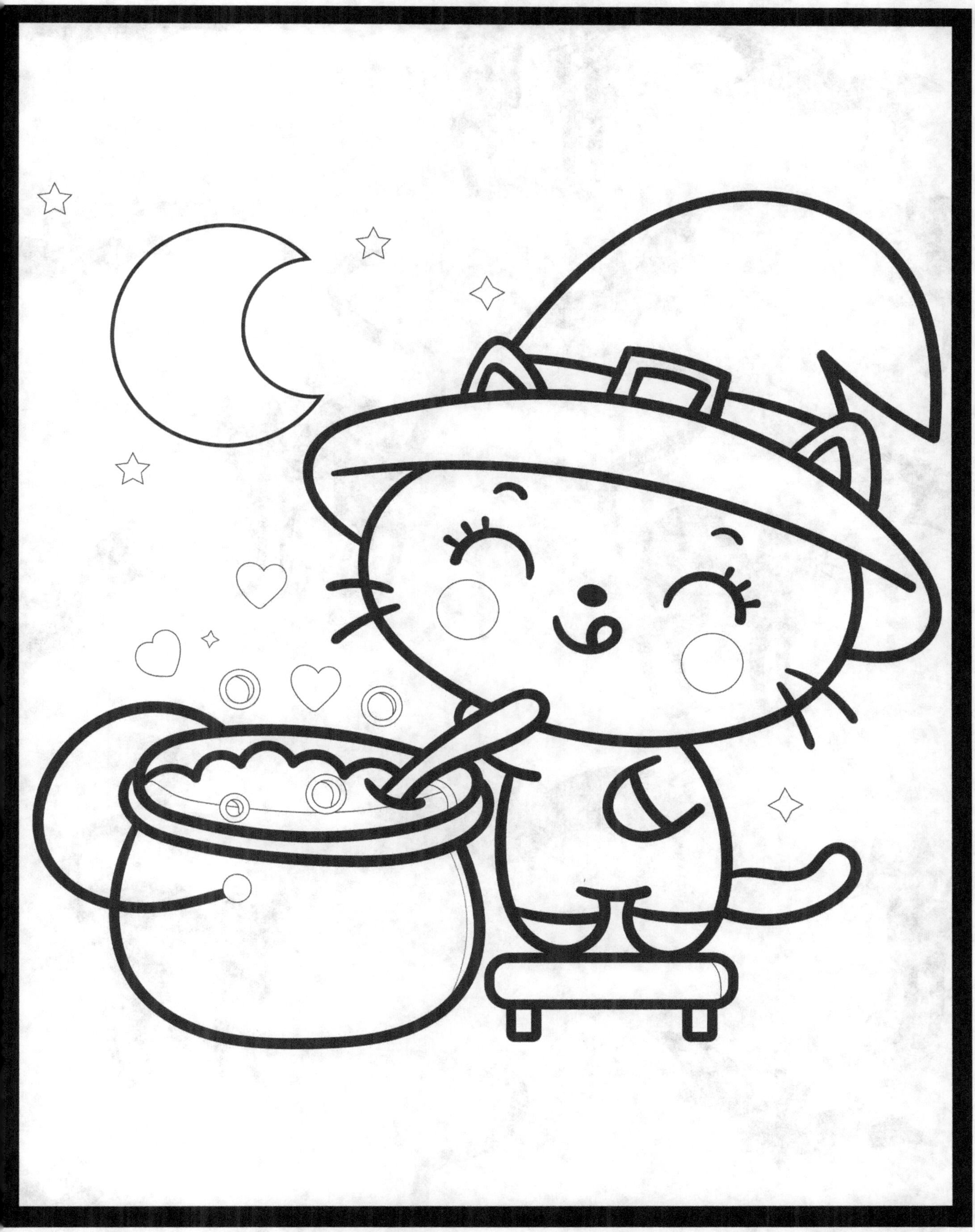

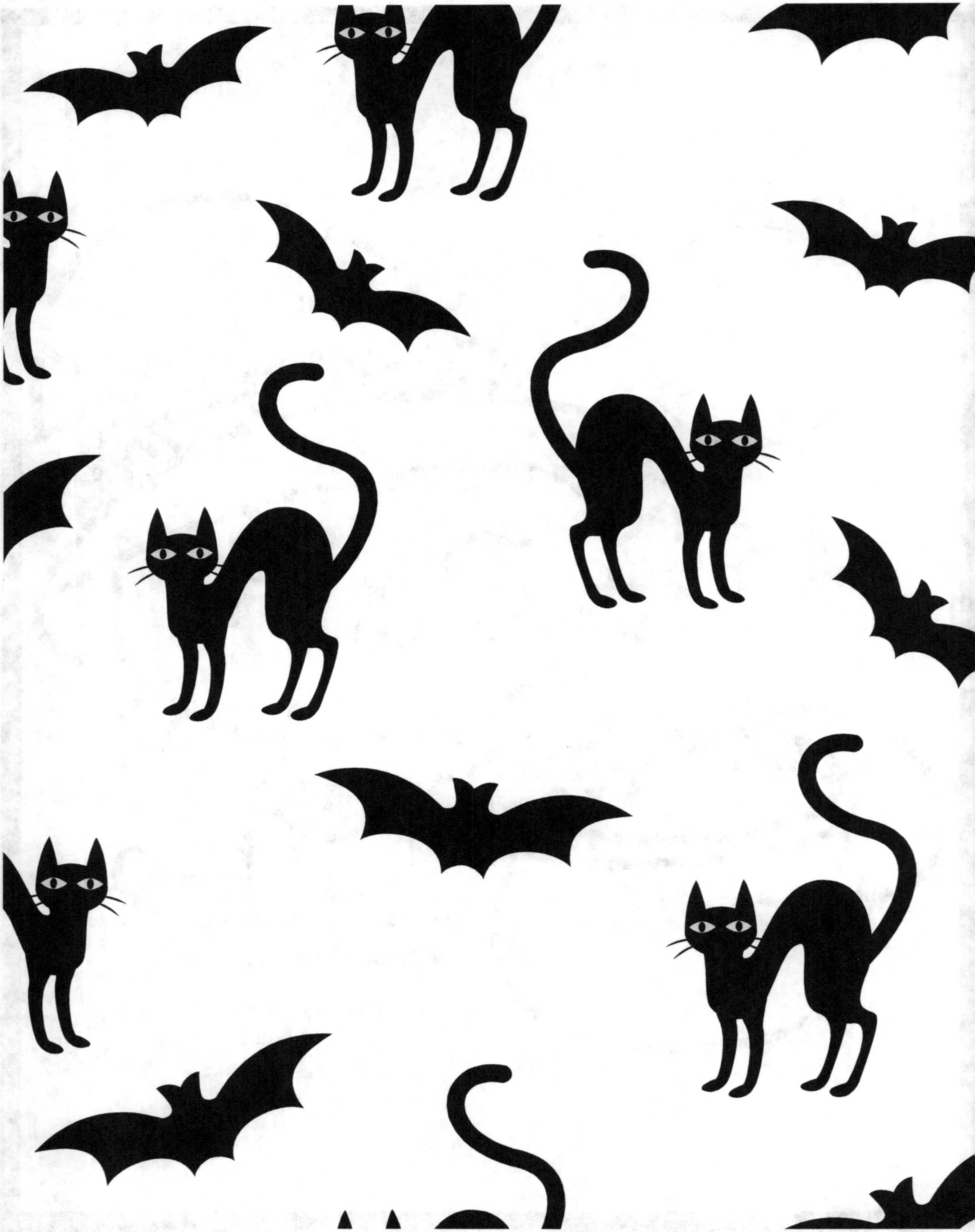

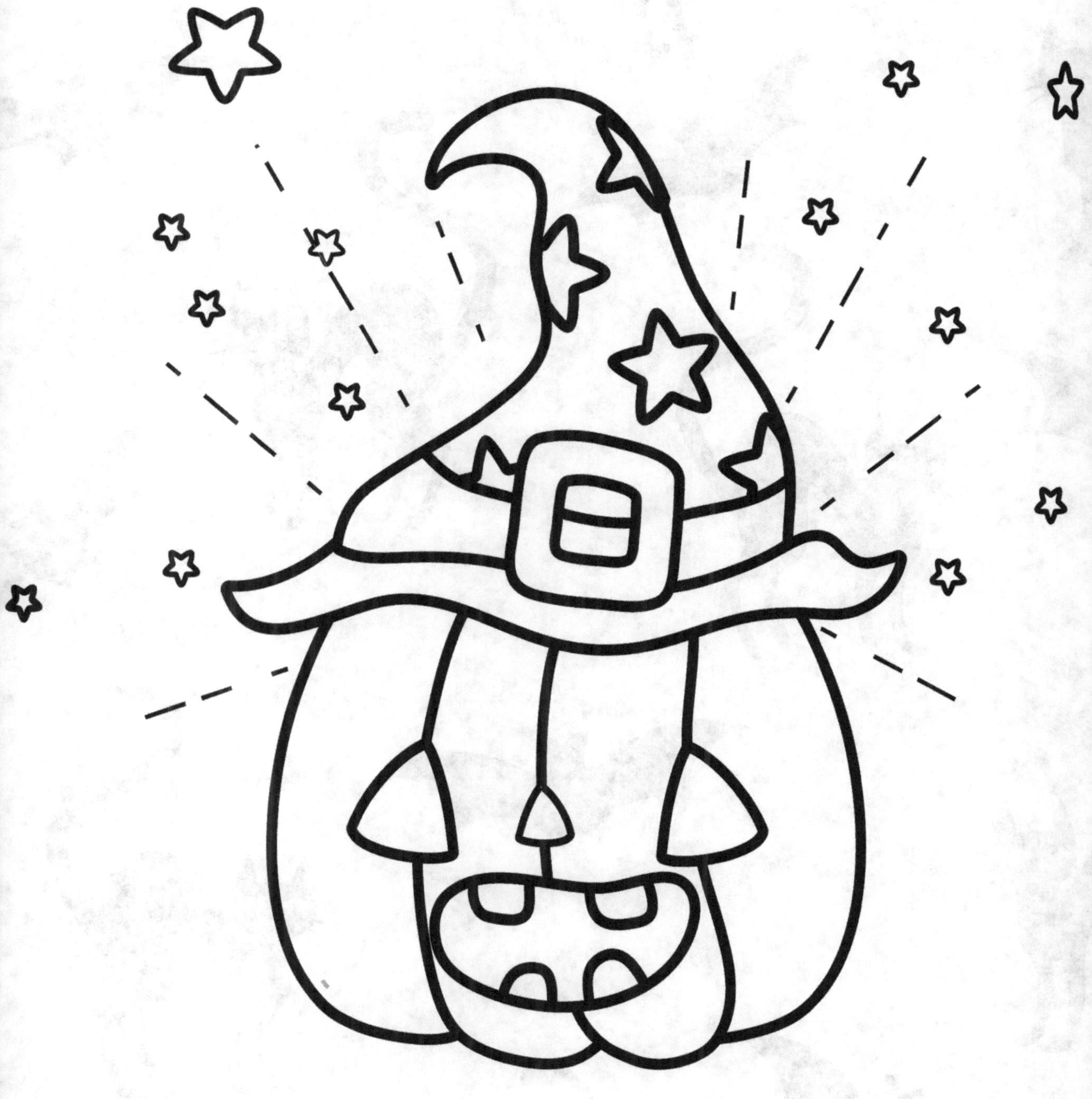

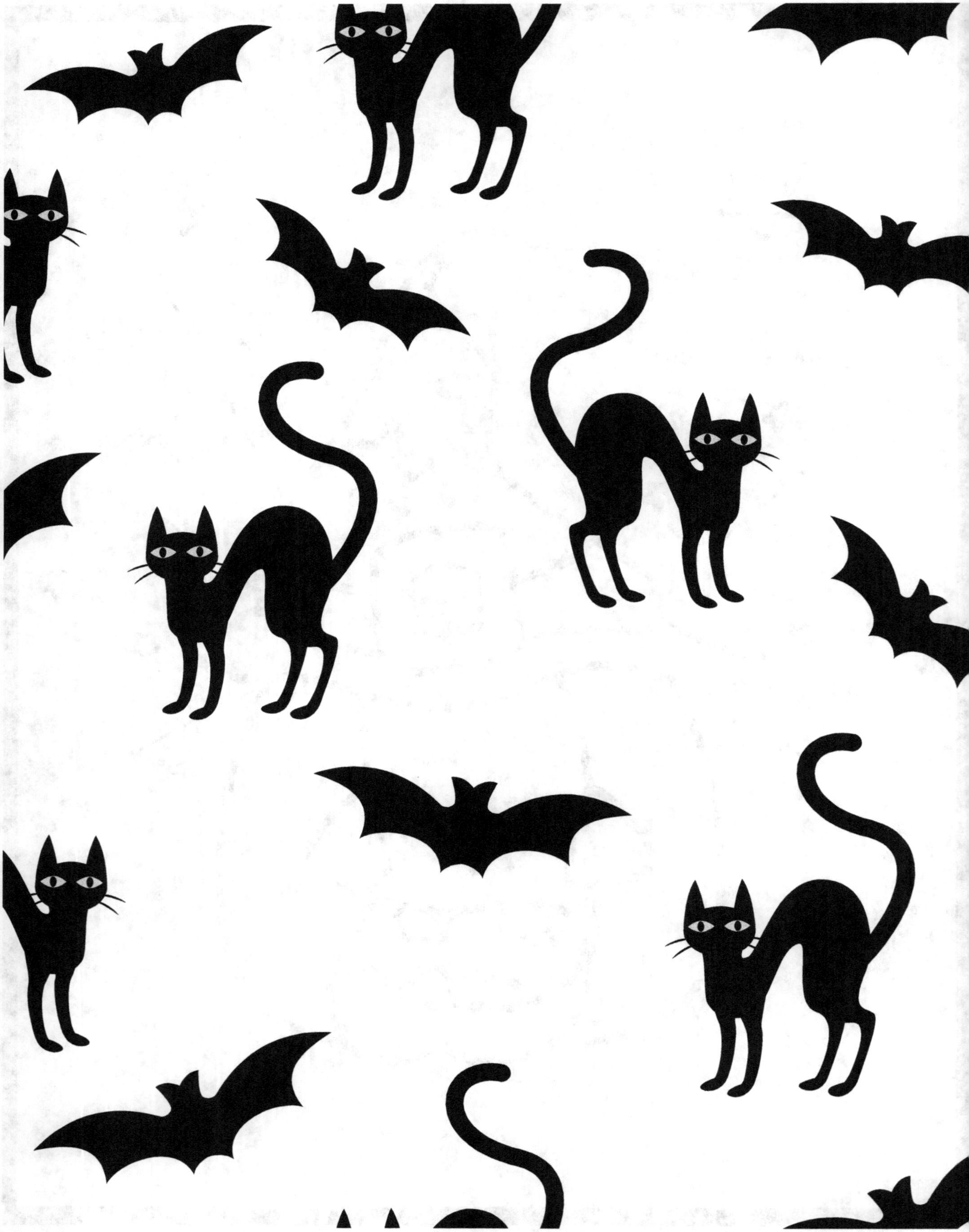

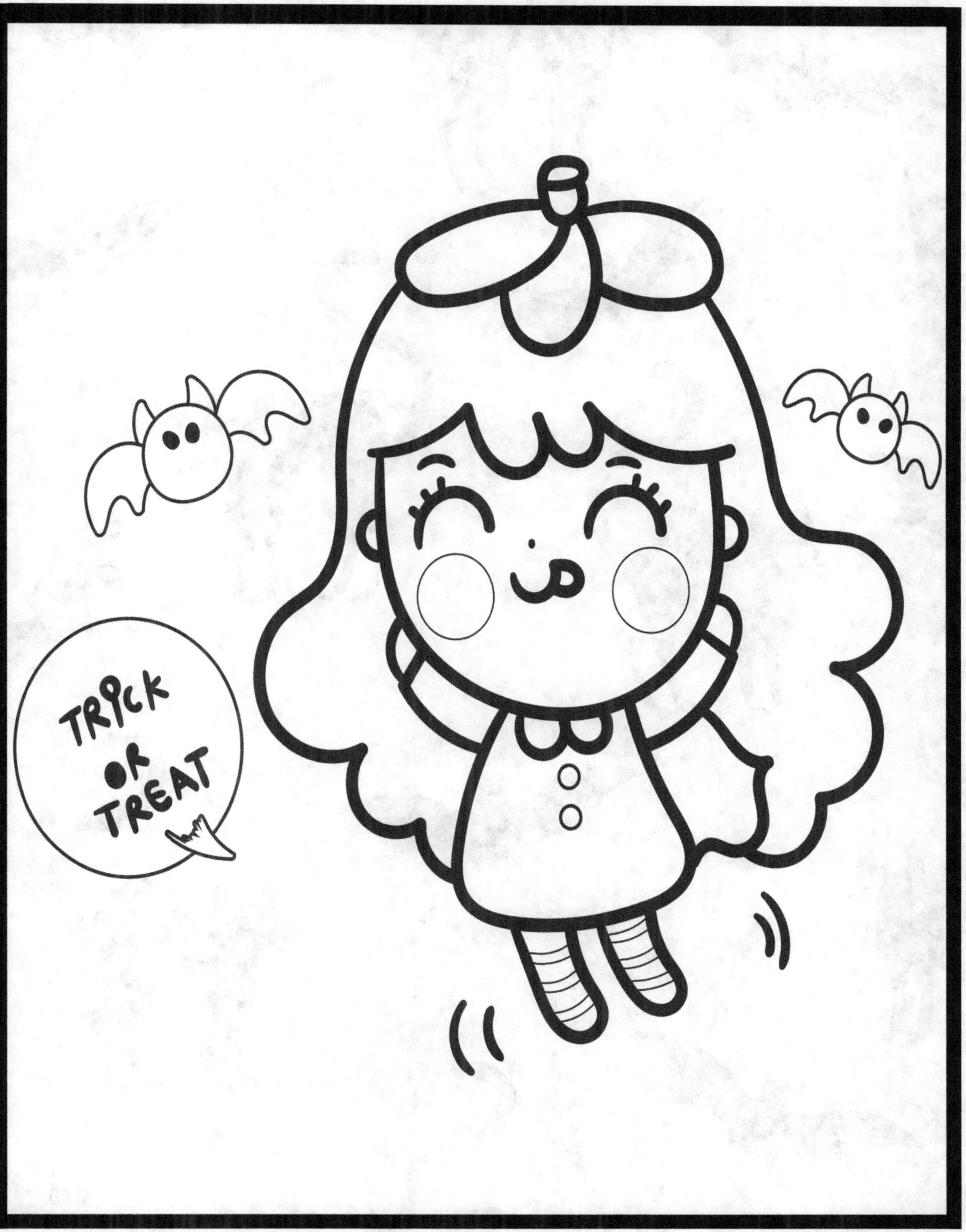
TRICK
OR
TREAT

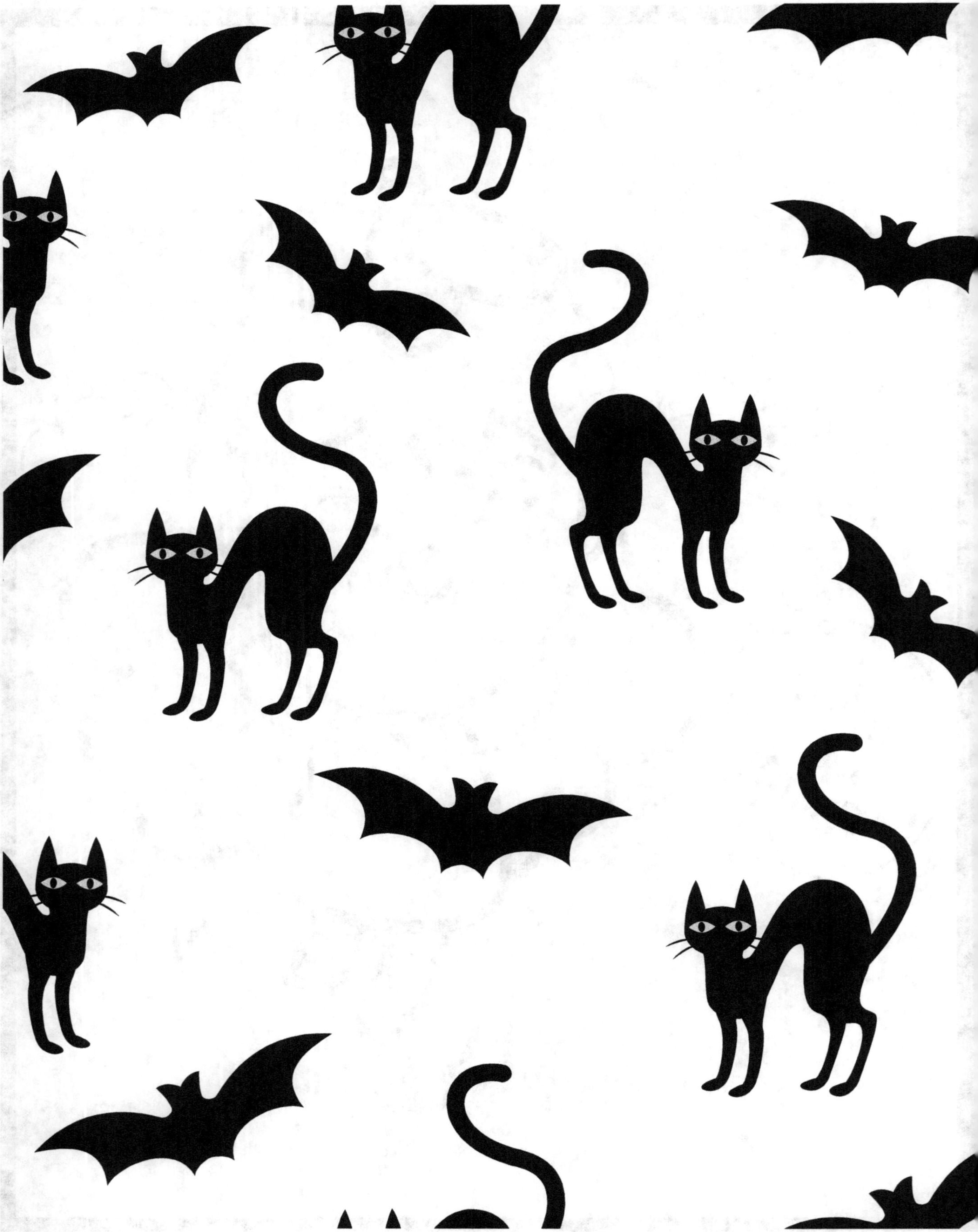

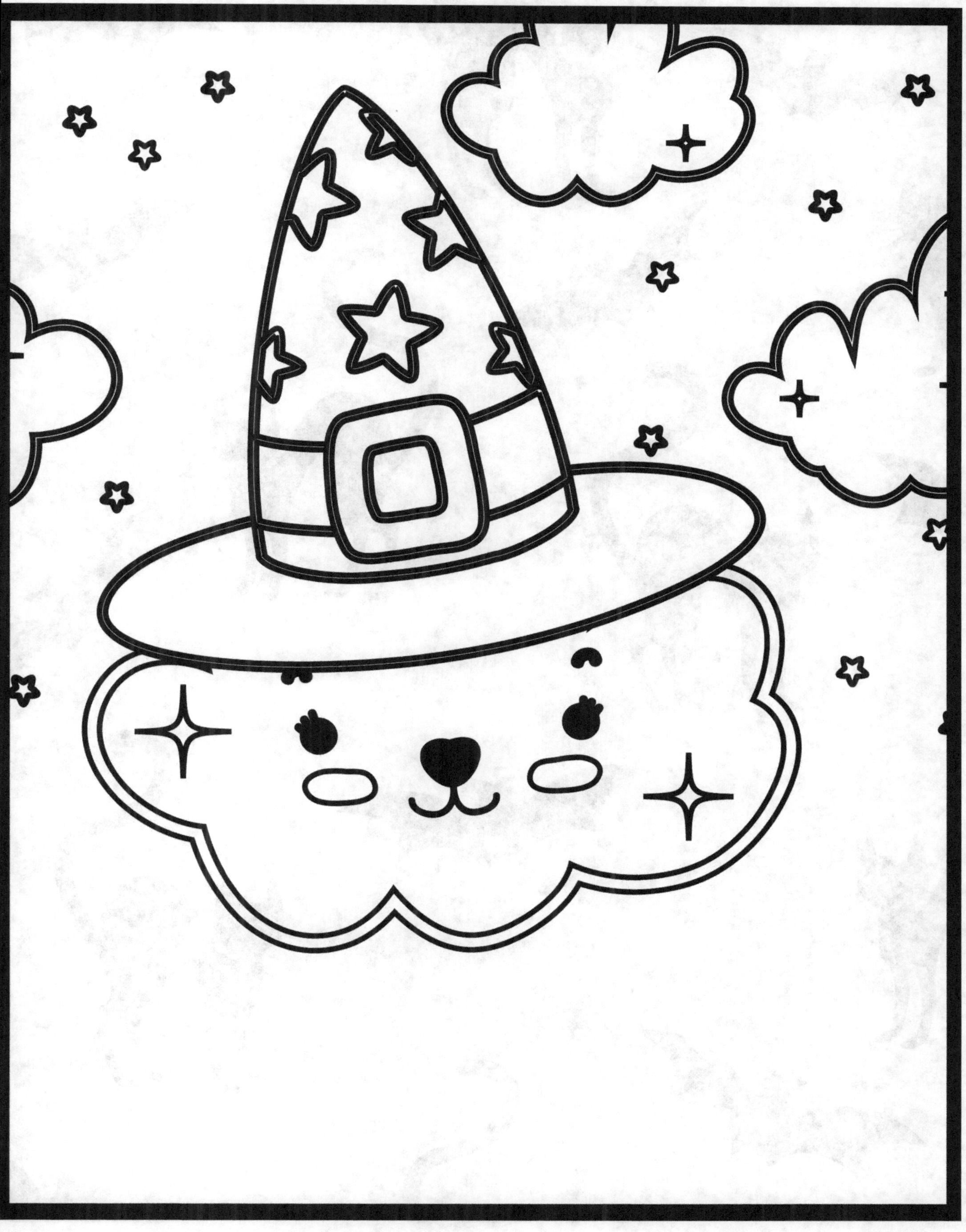

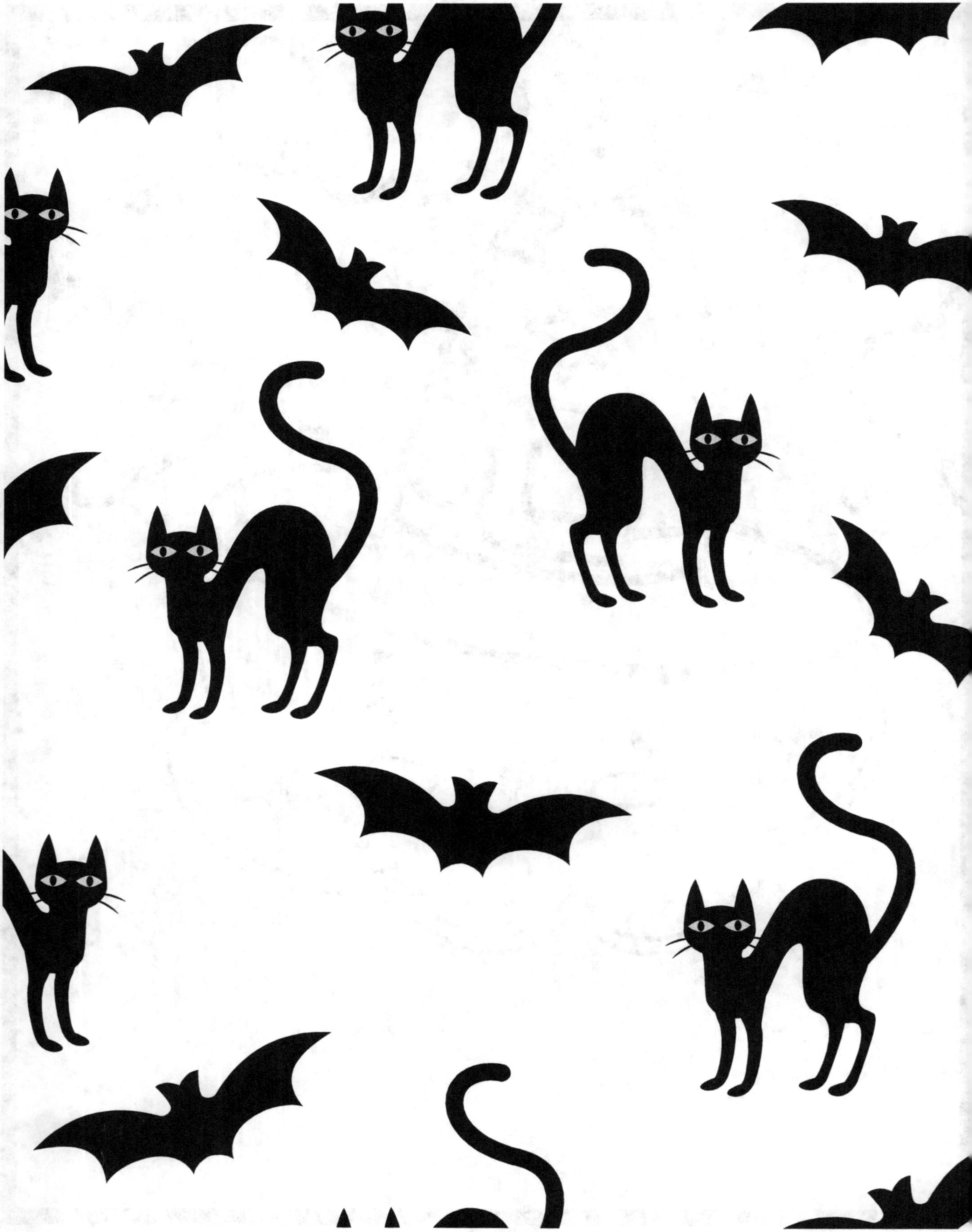

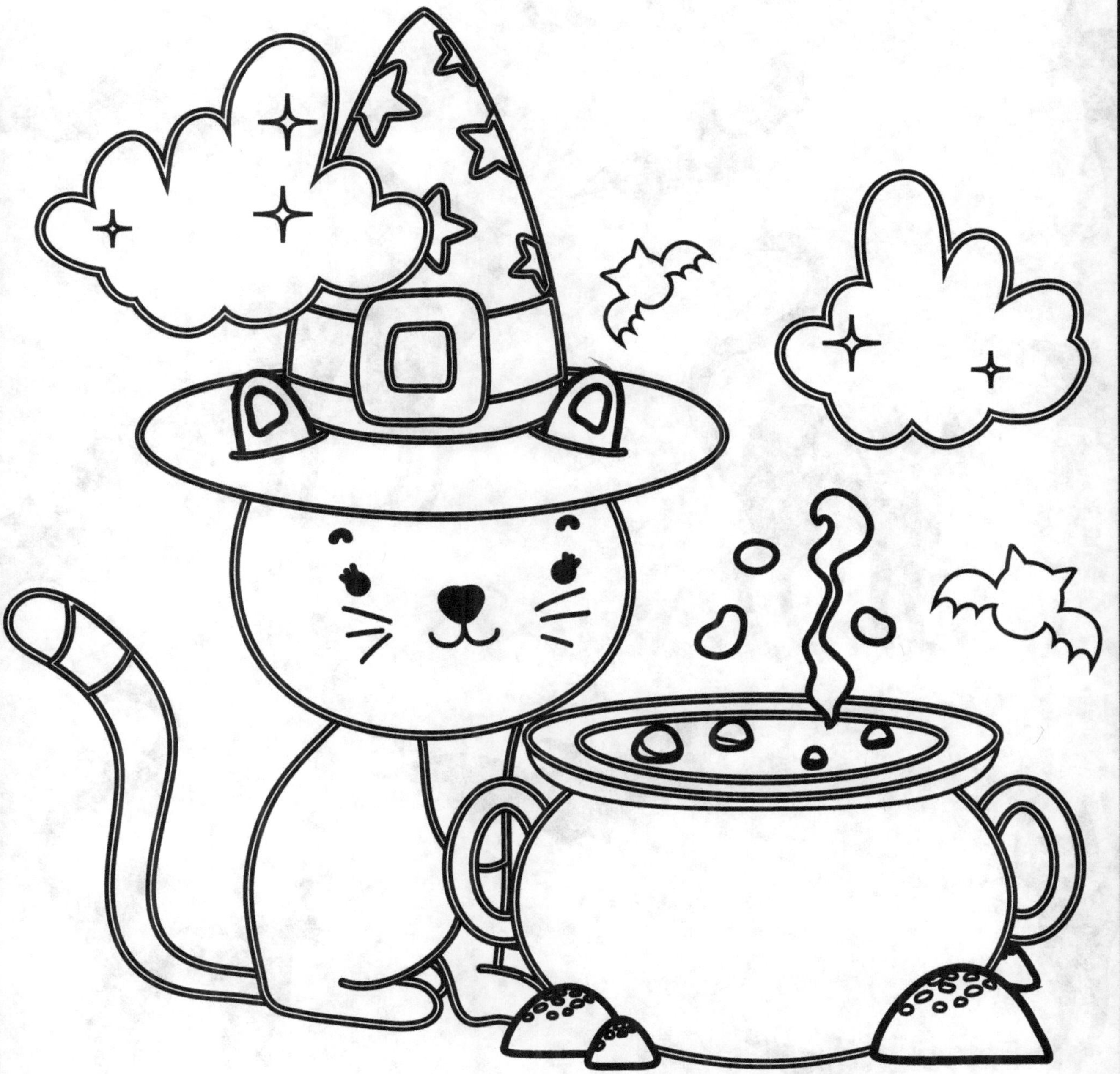

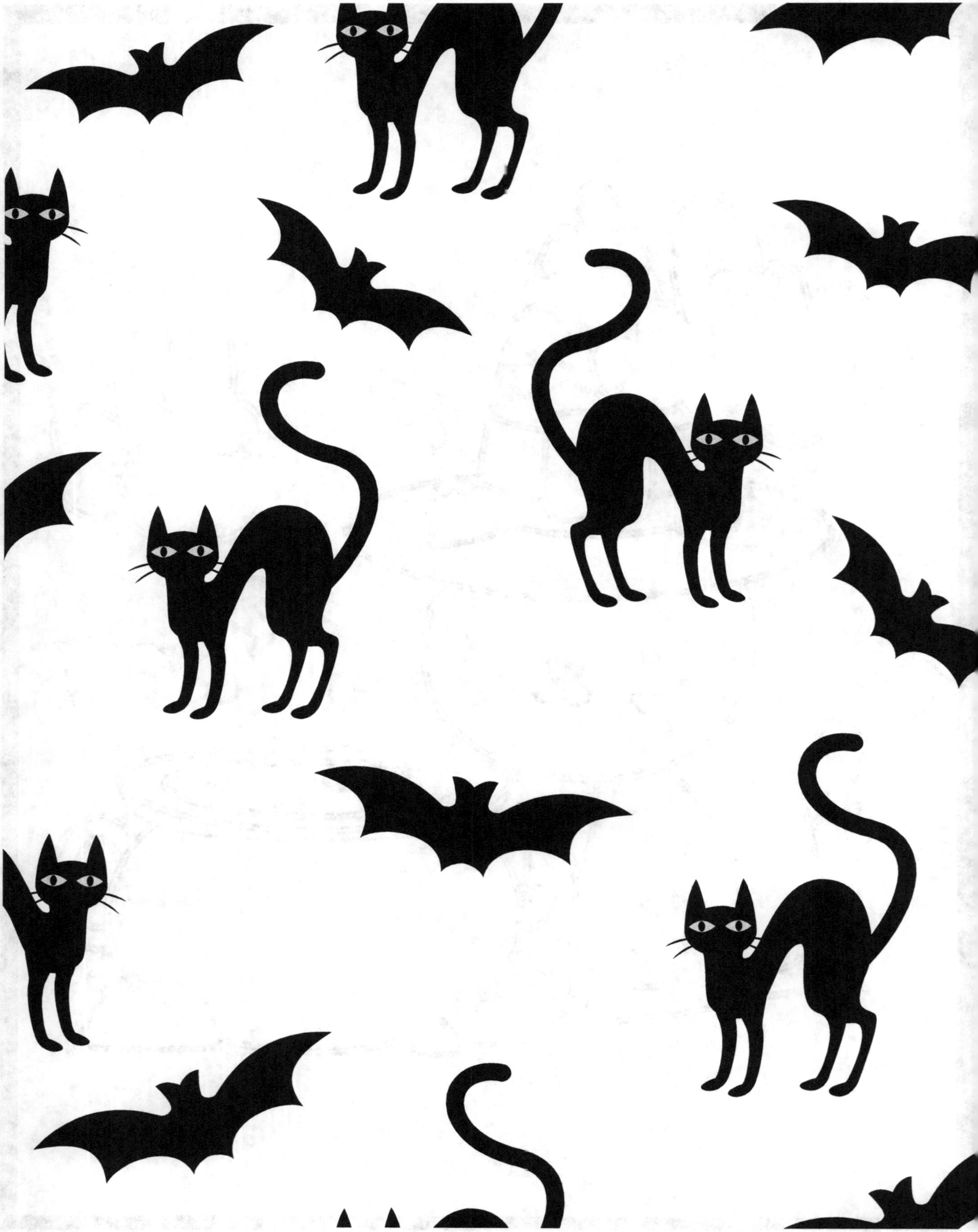

Halloween
Party

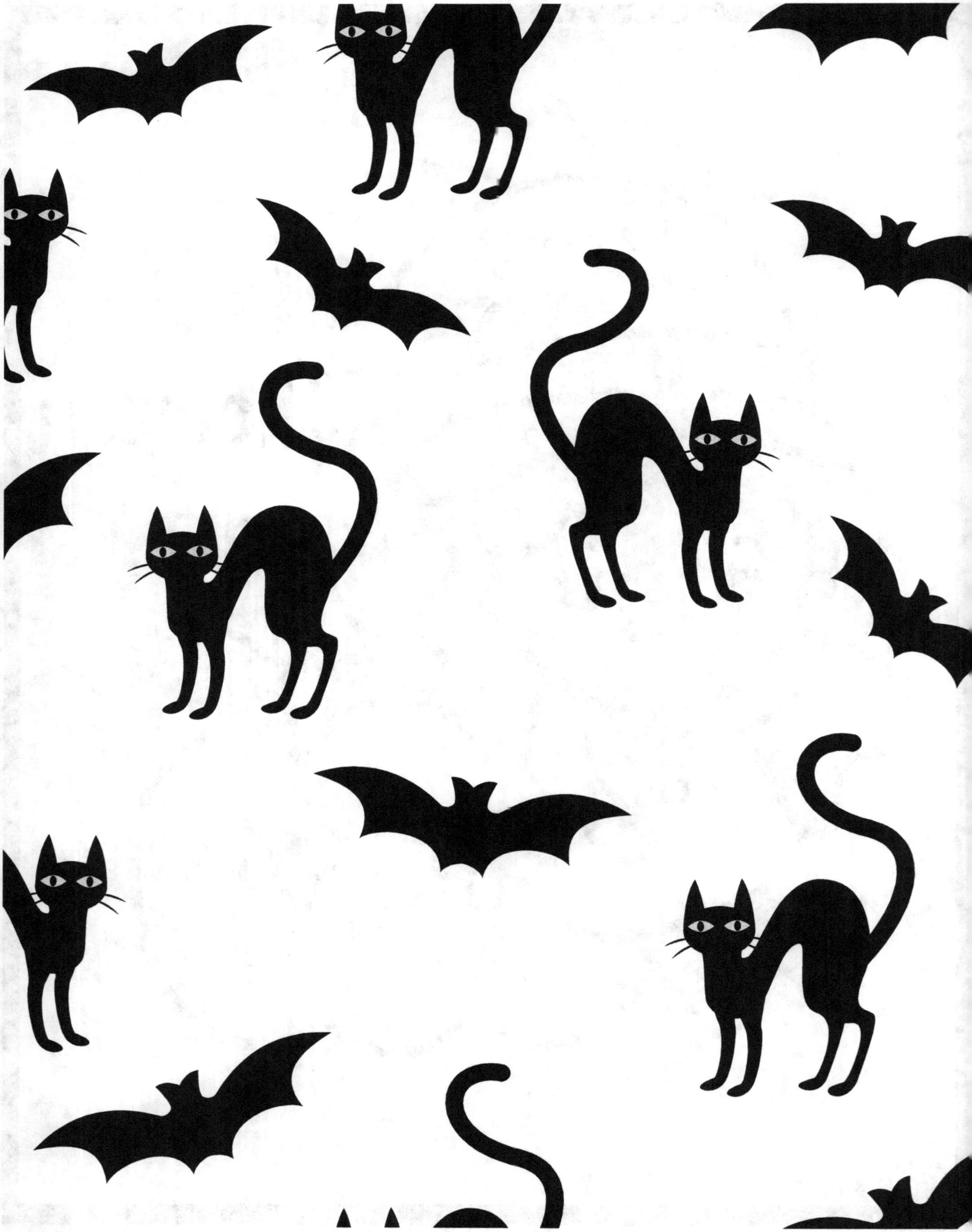

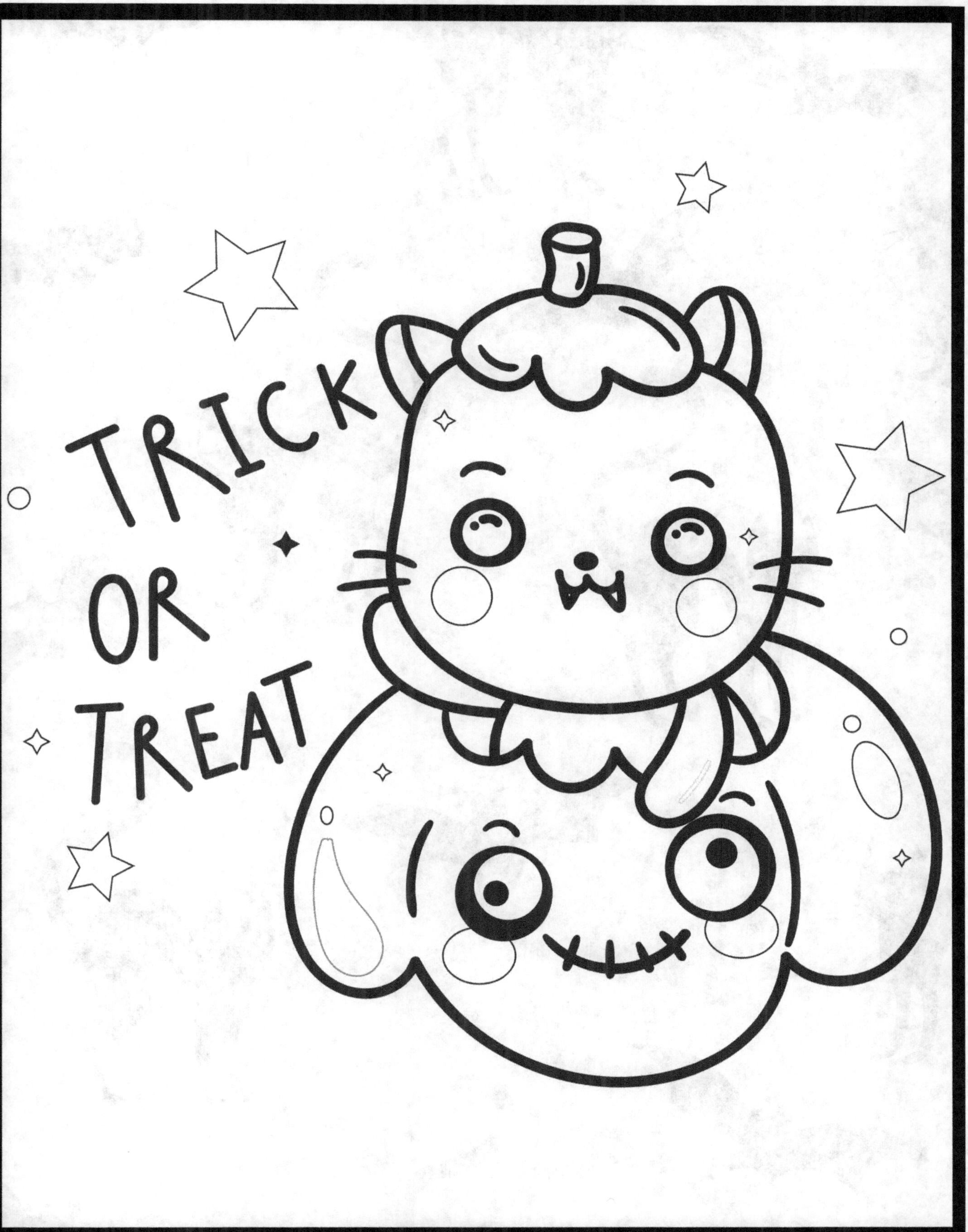
TRICK
OR
TREAT

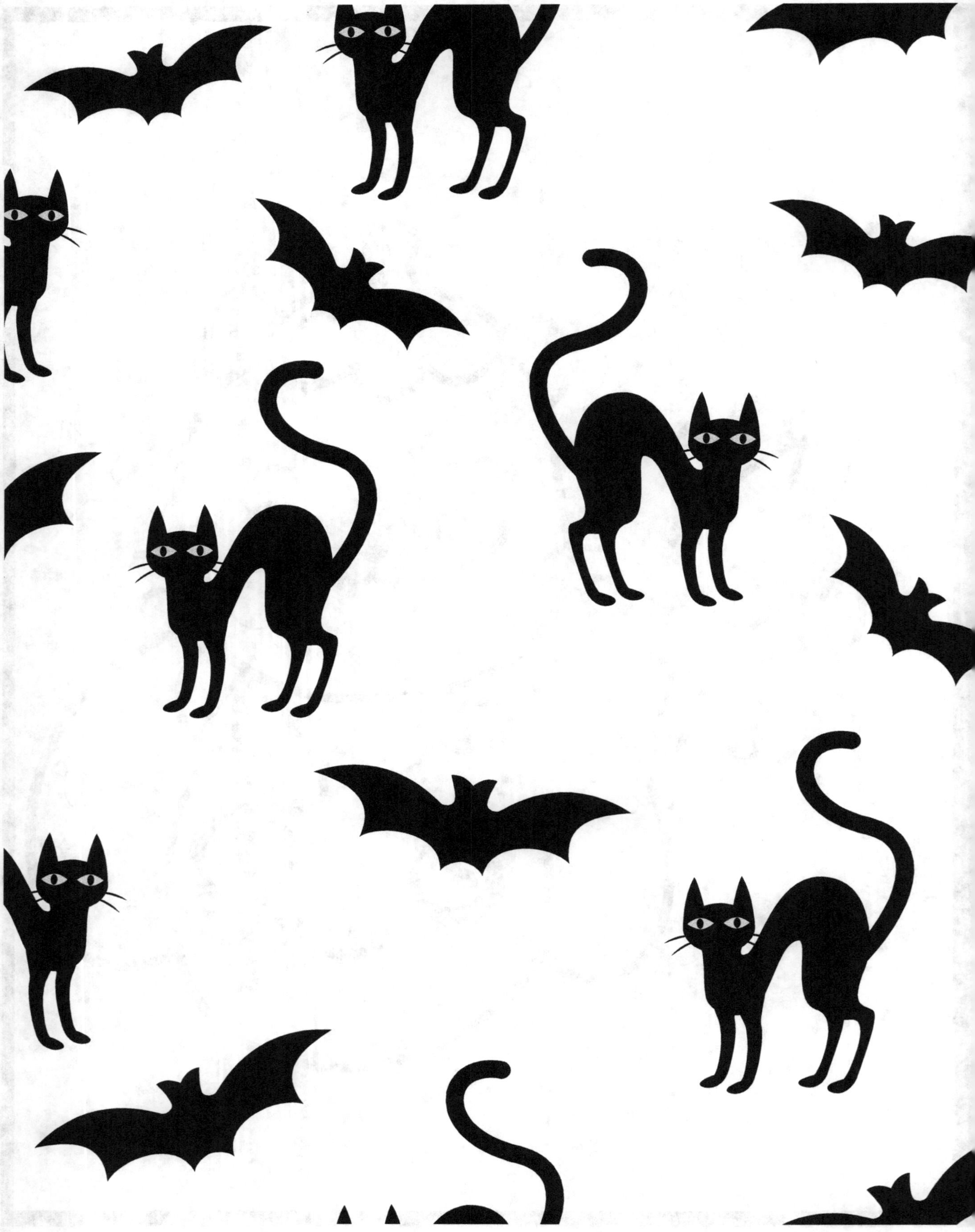

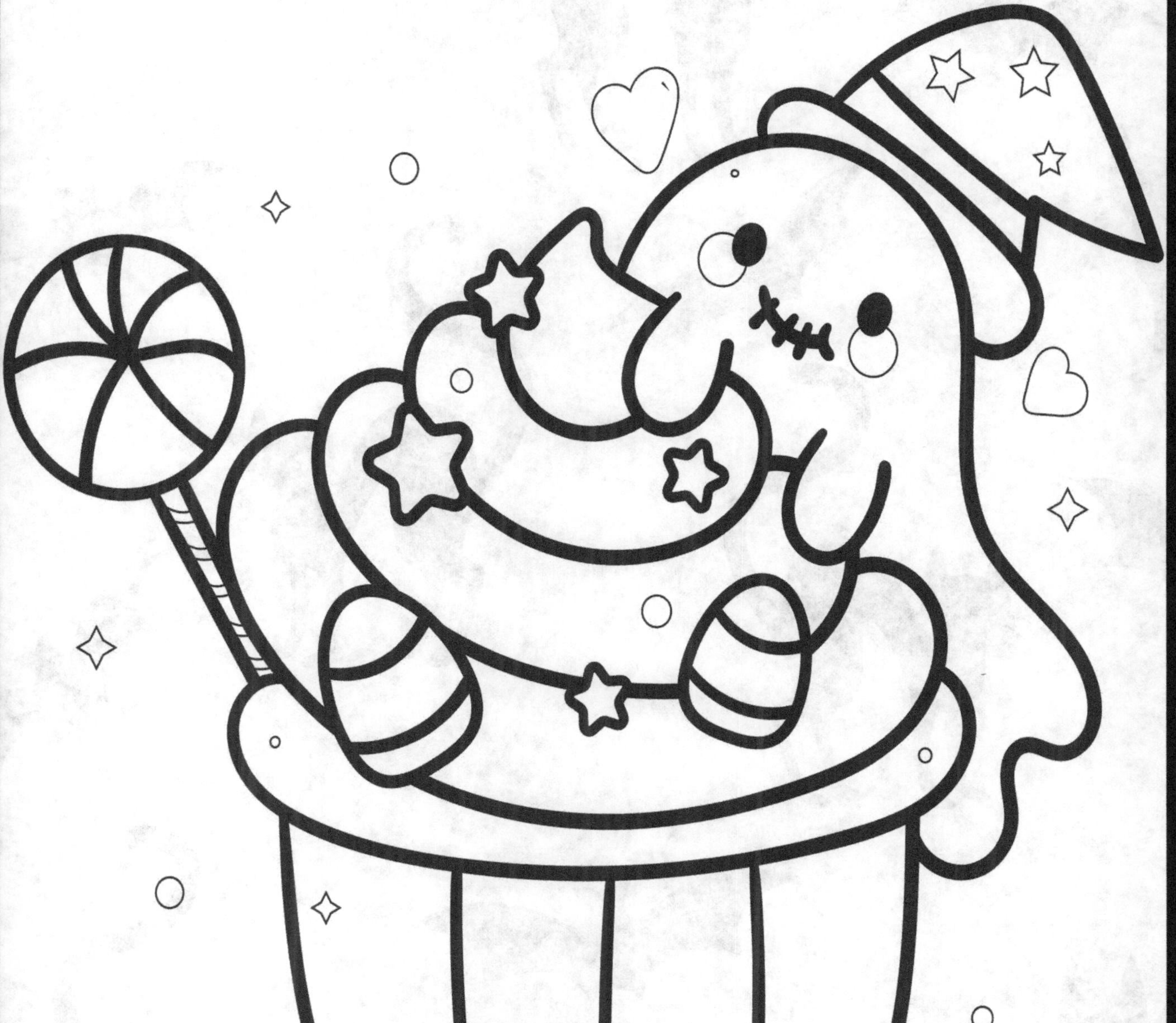

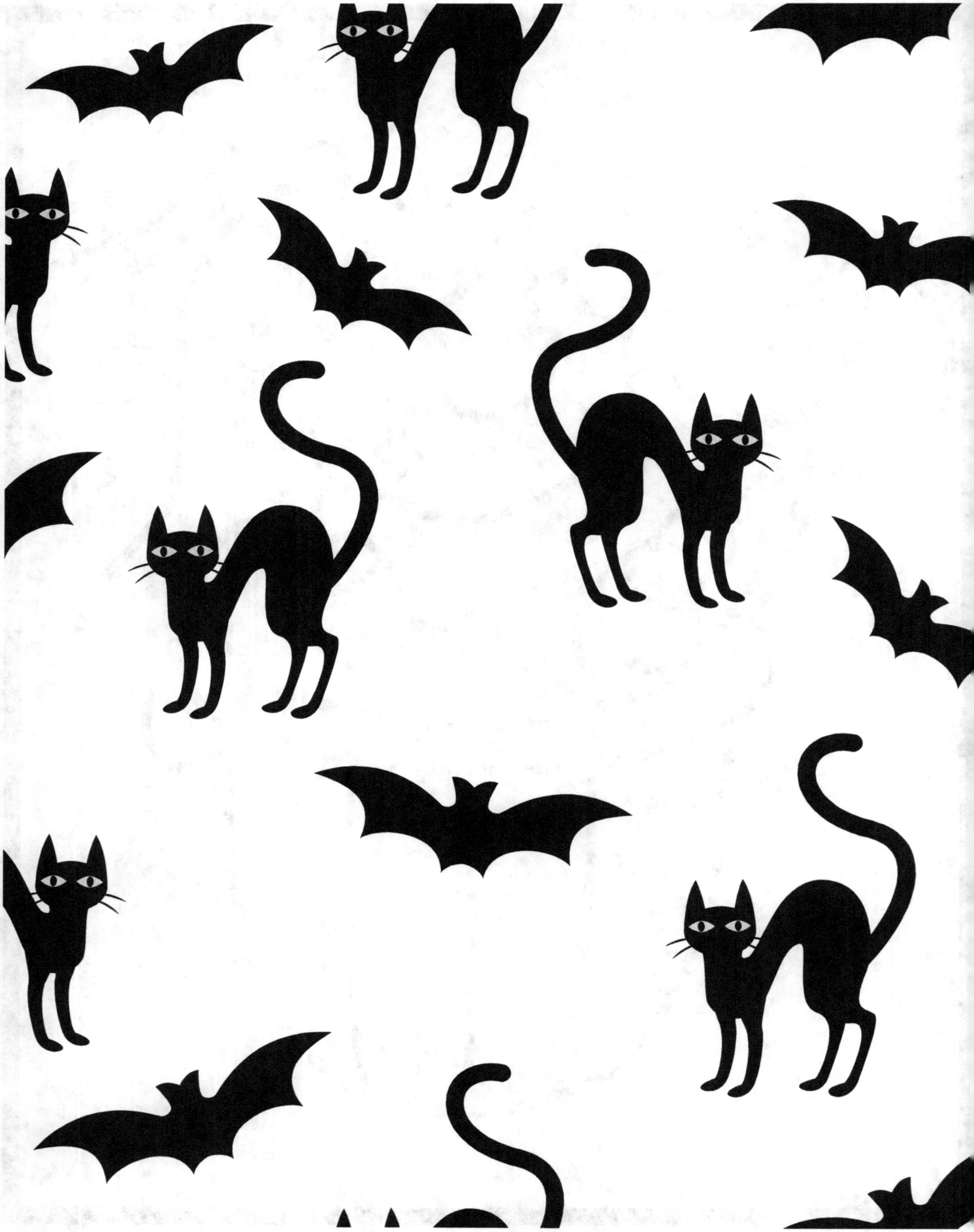

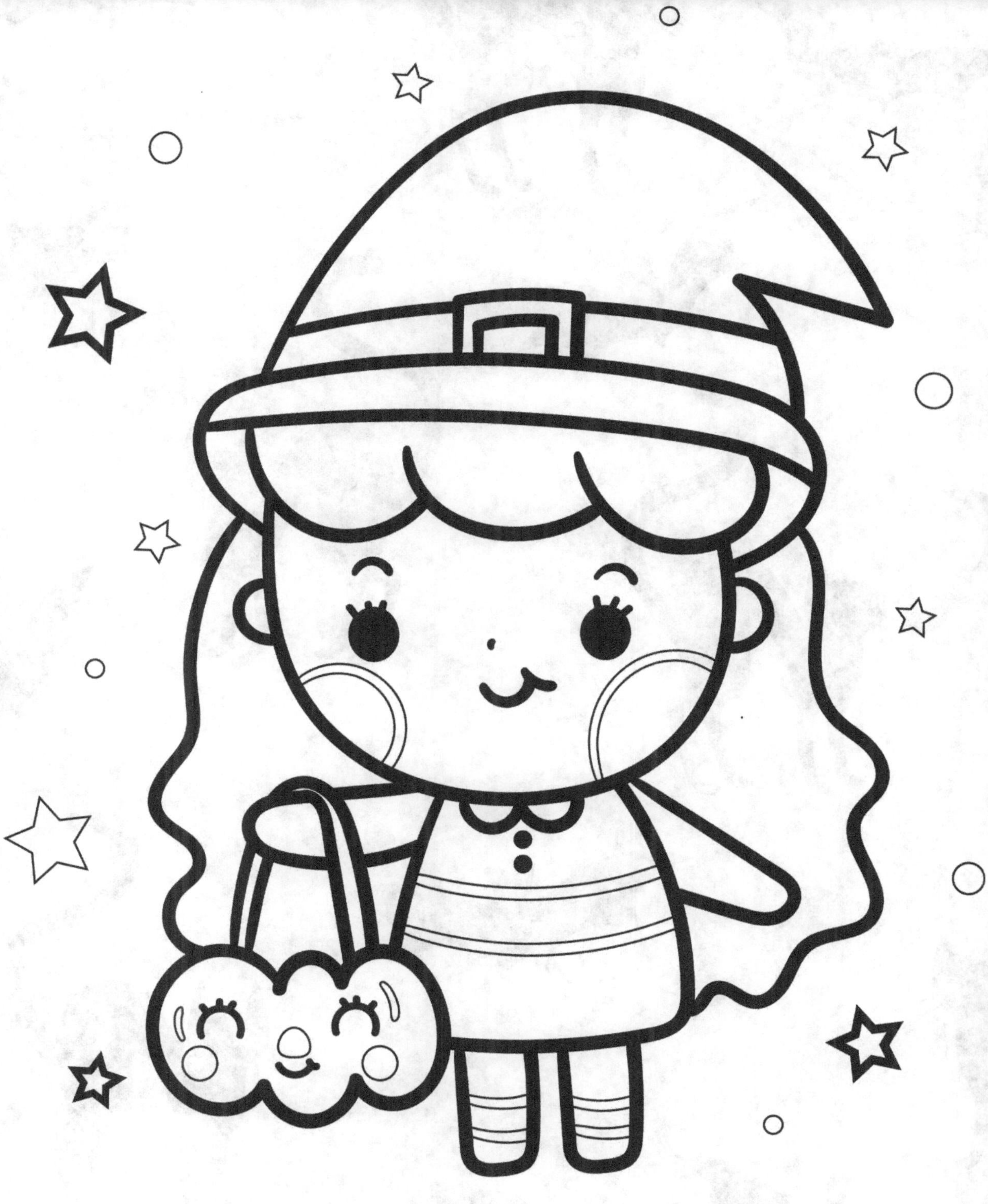

HALLOWEEN

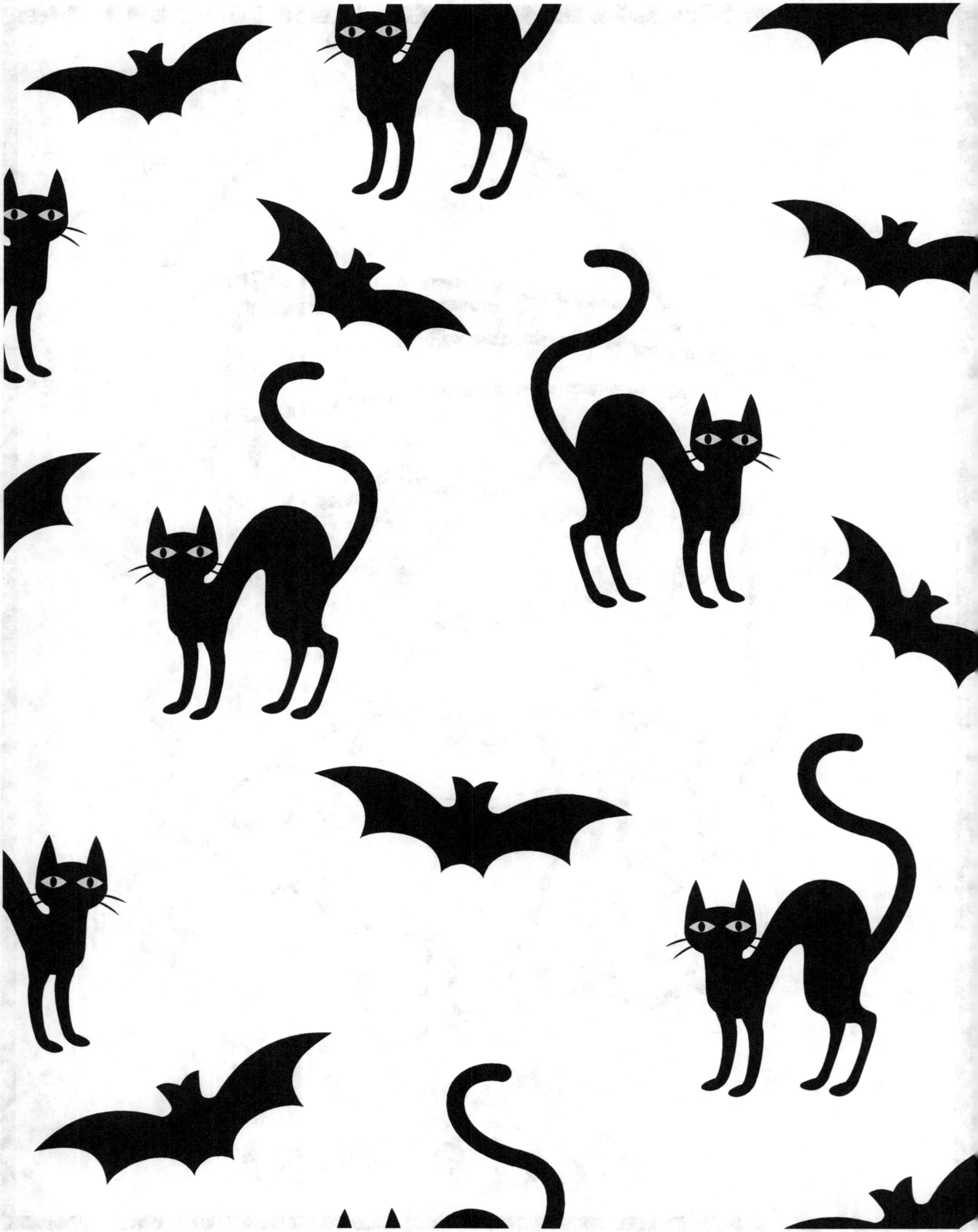

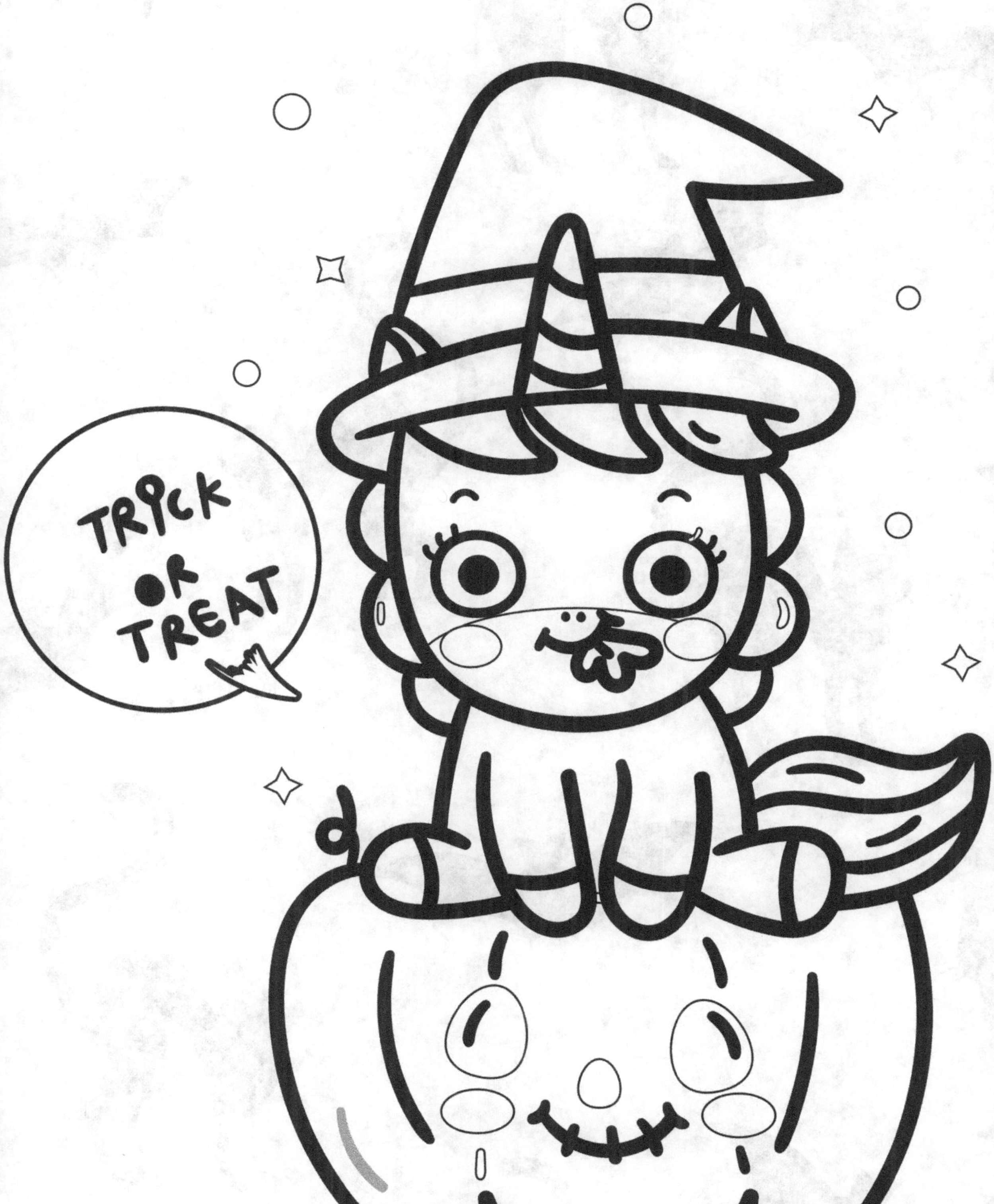
TRICK
OR
TREAT

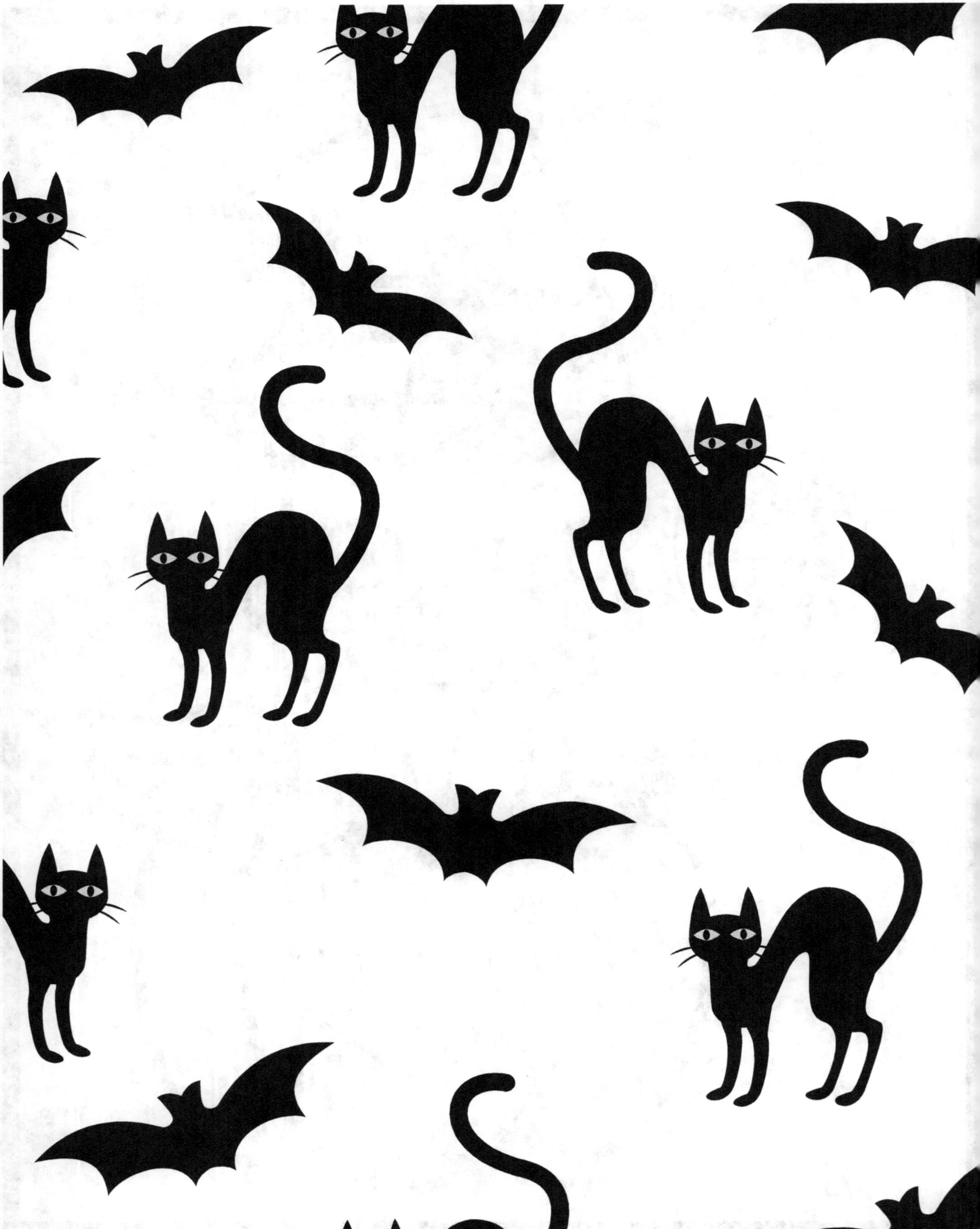

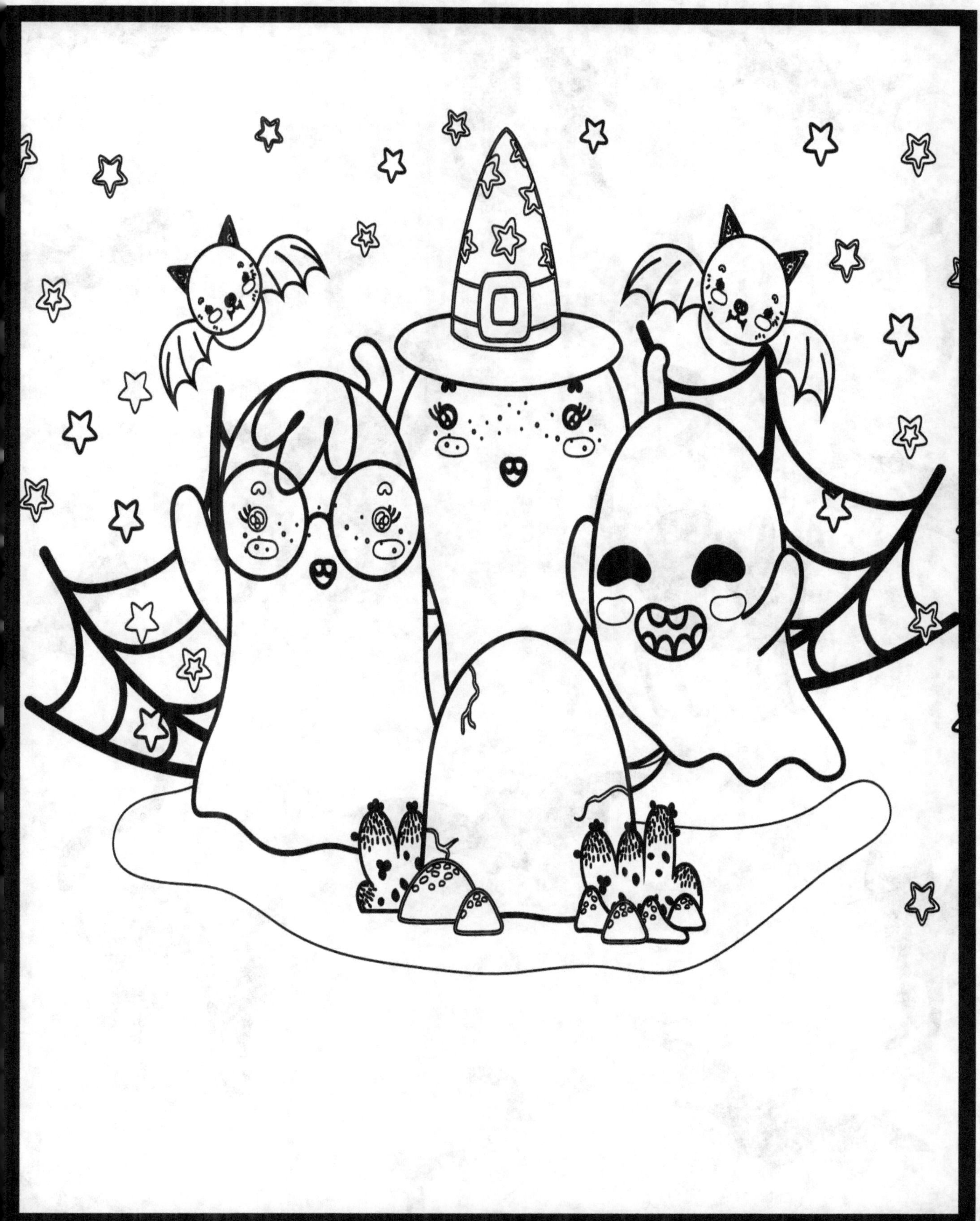

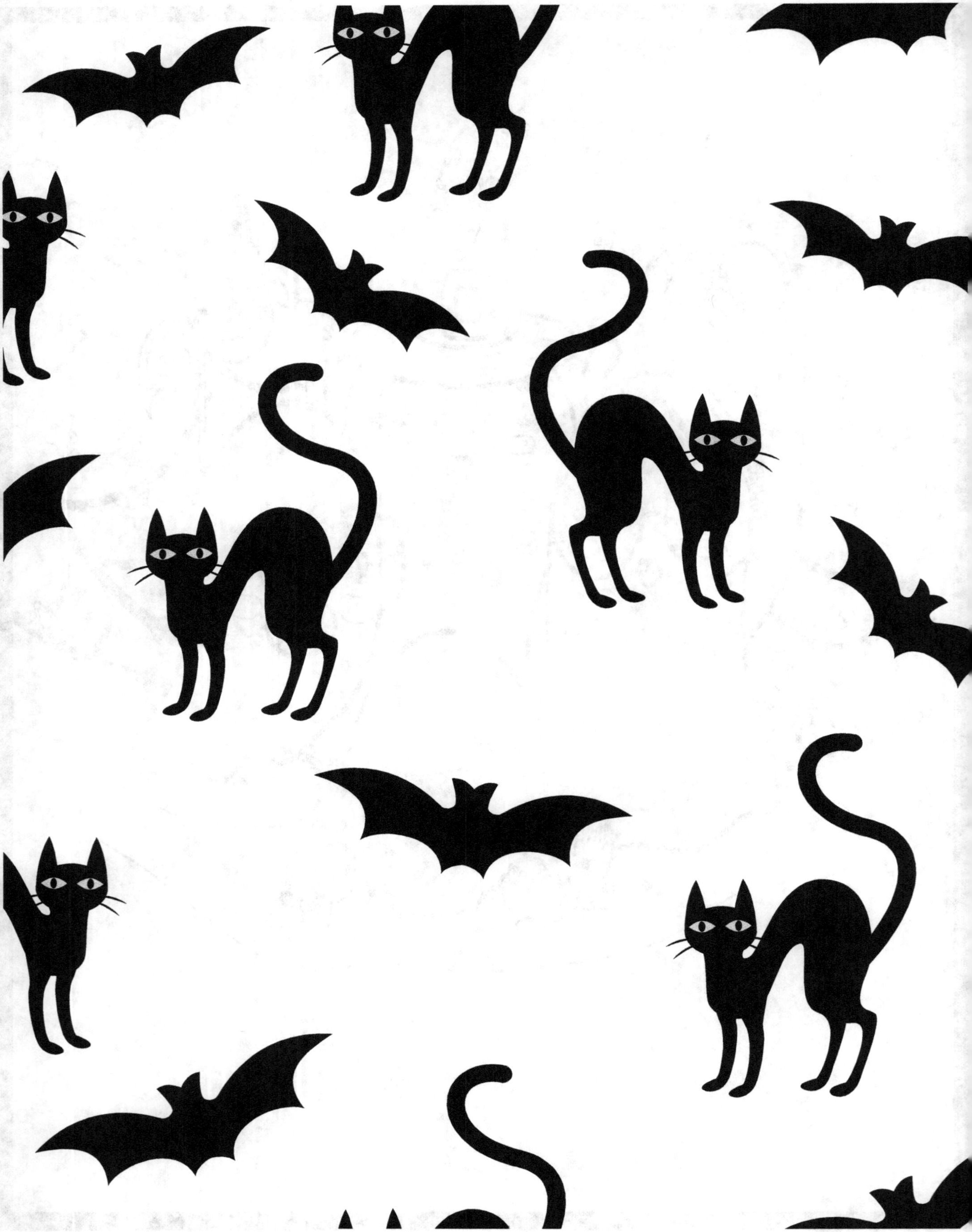

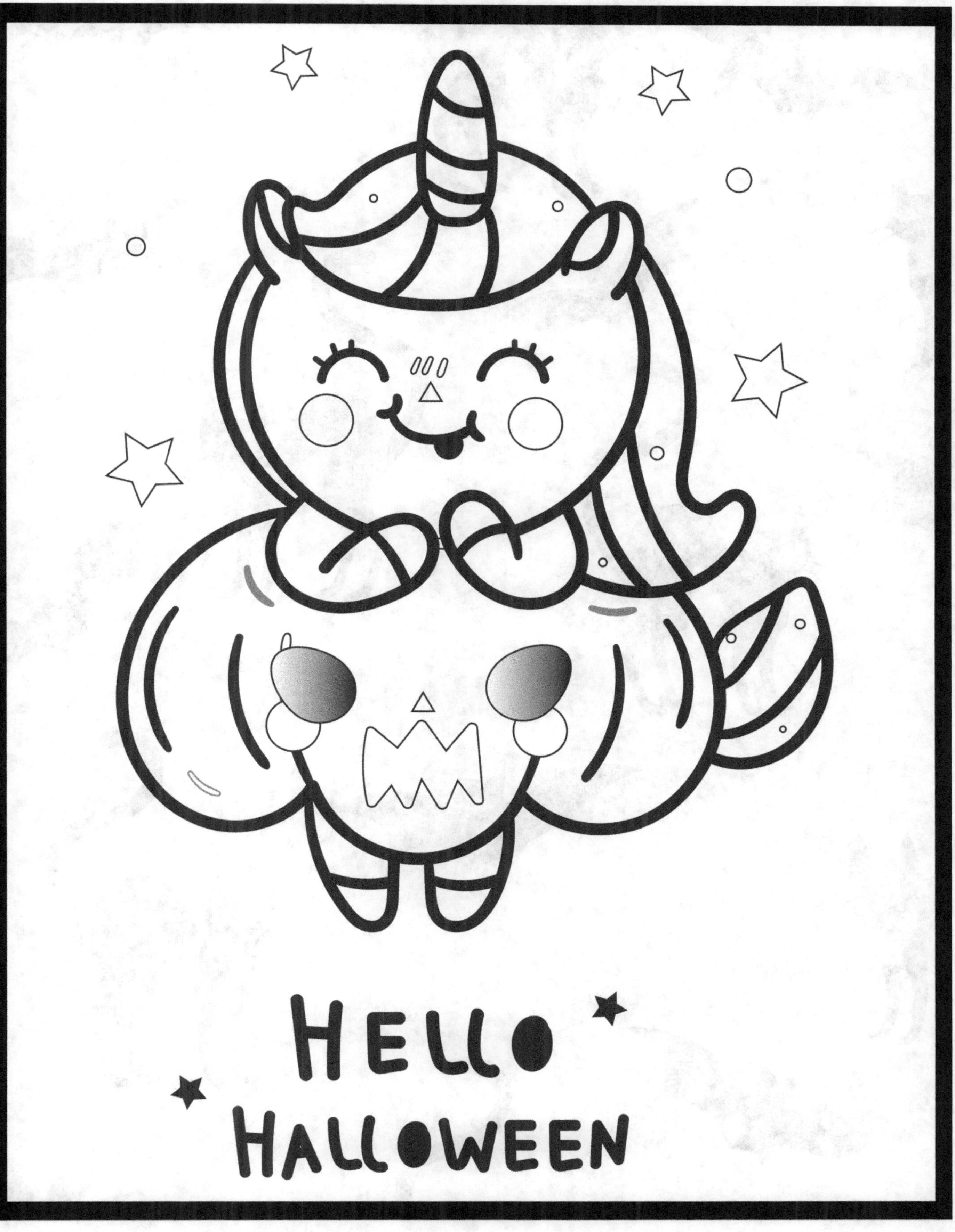
HELLO
HALLOWEEN

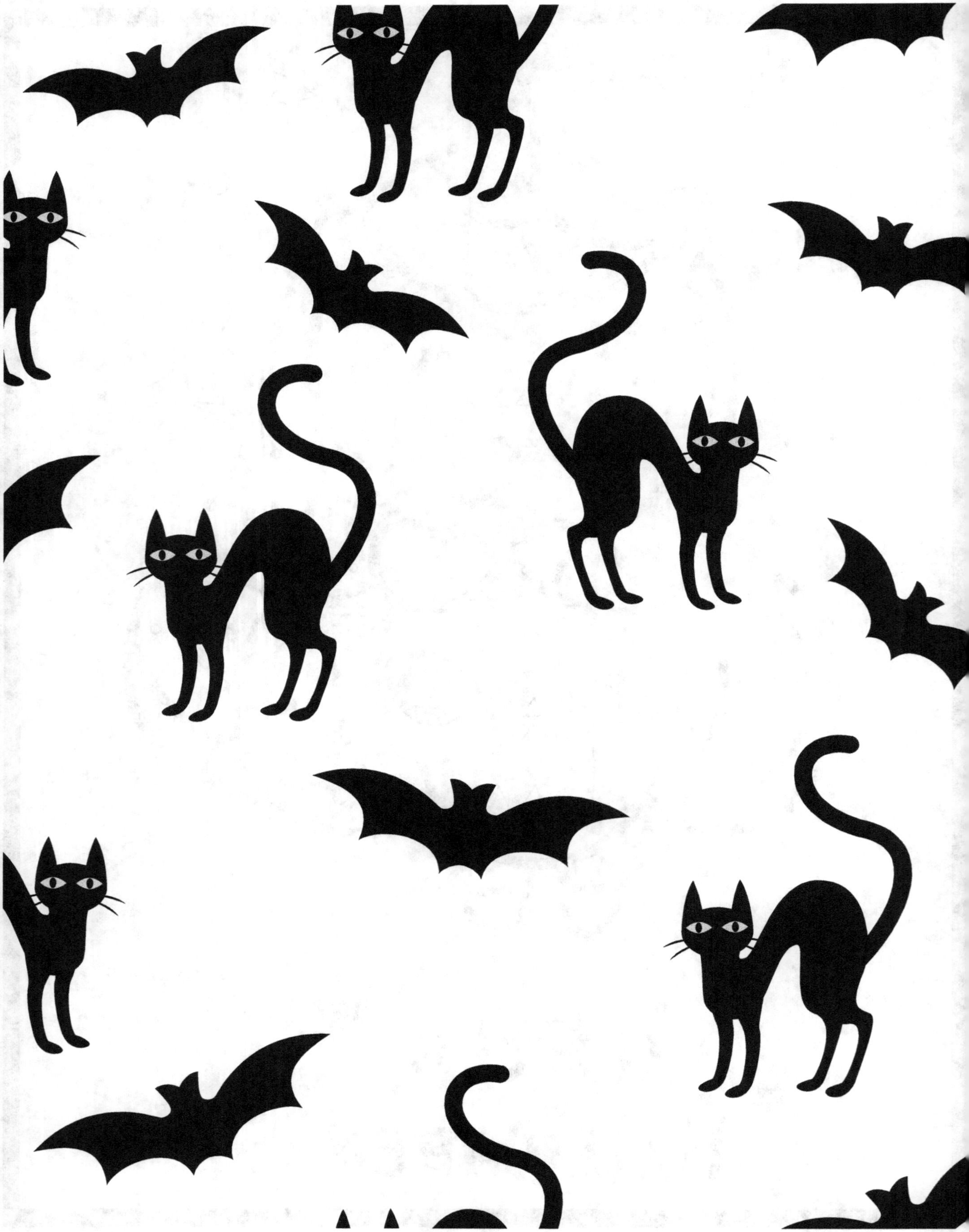

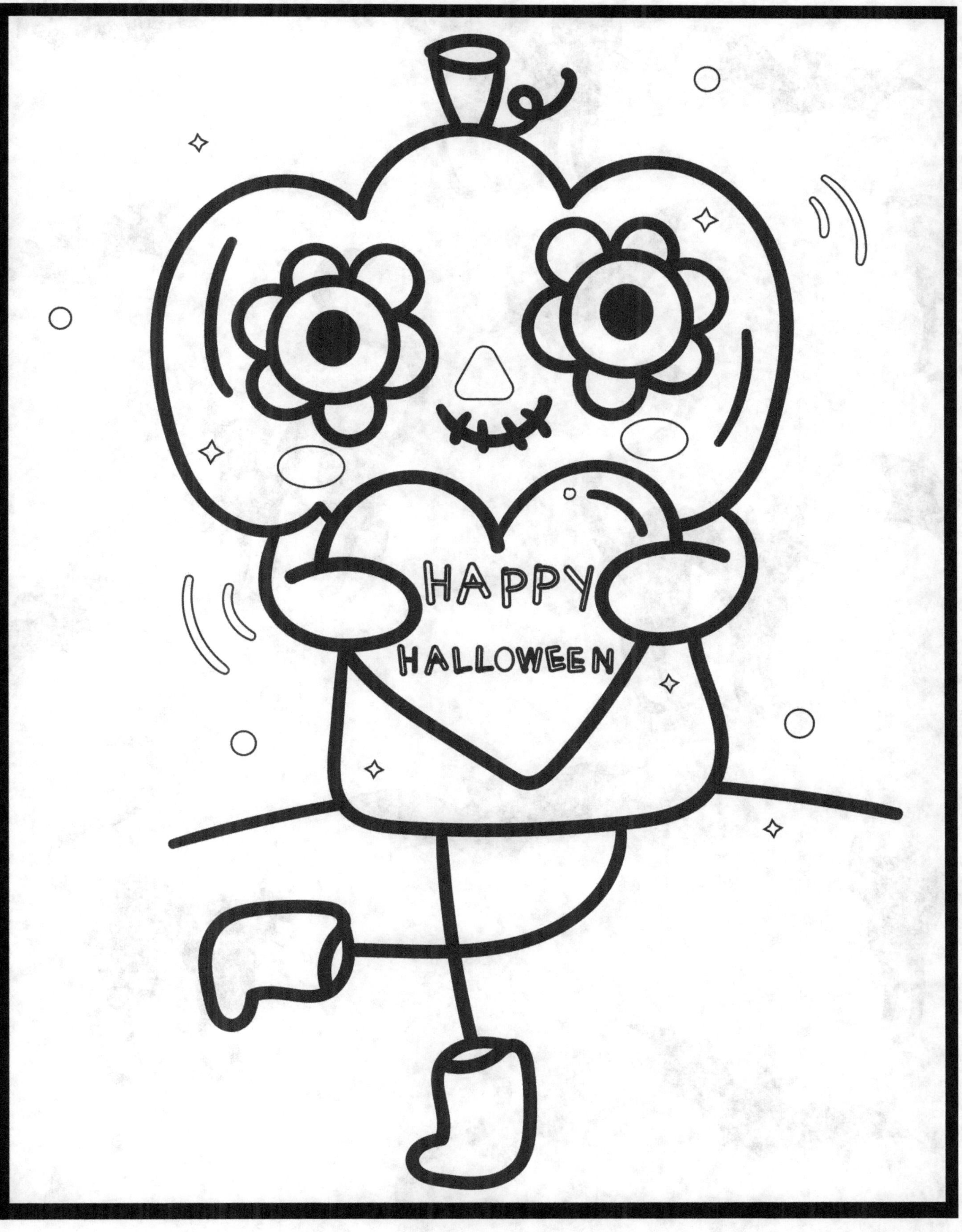
HAPPY
HALLOWEEN

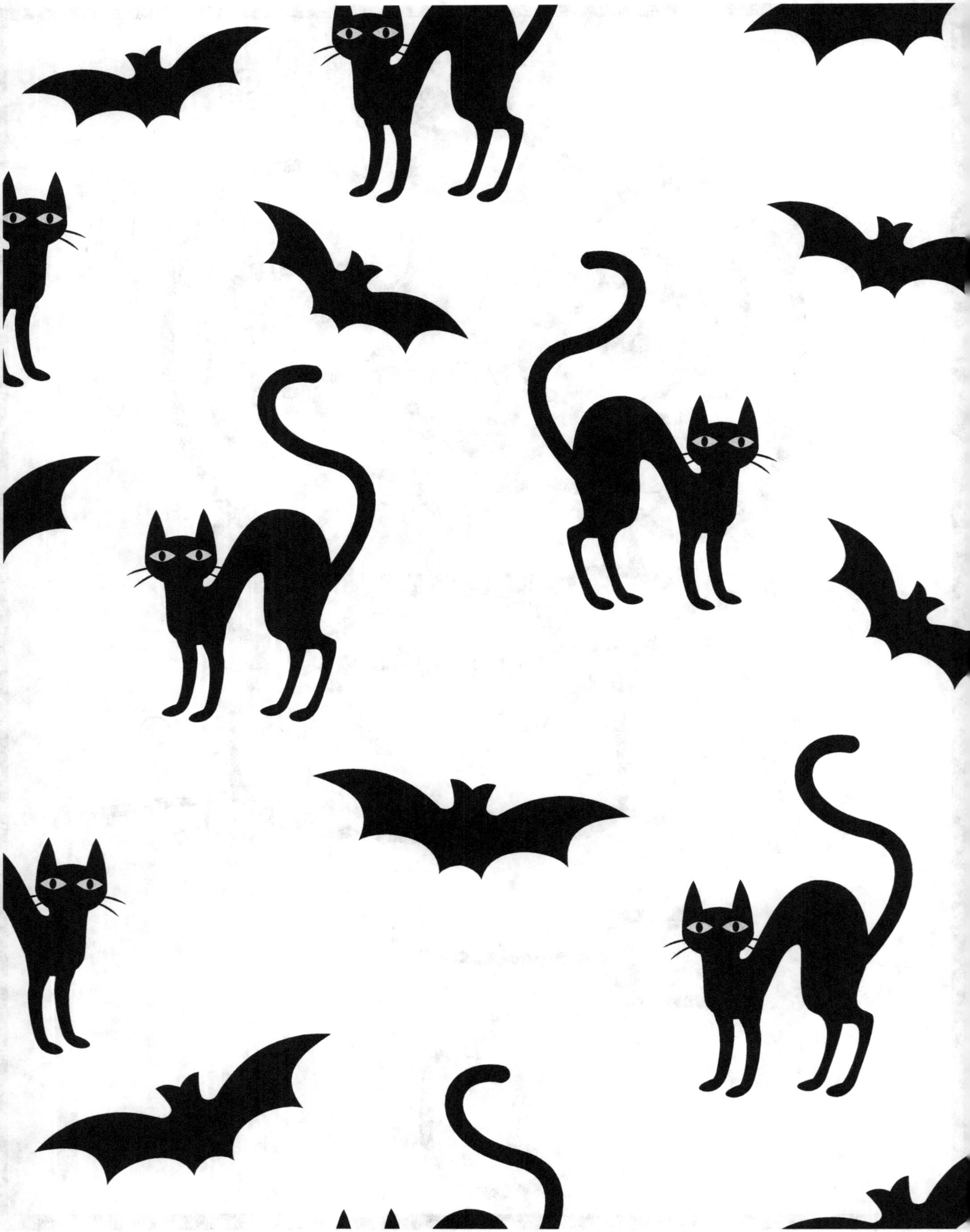

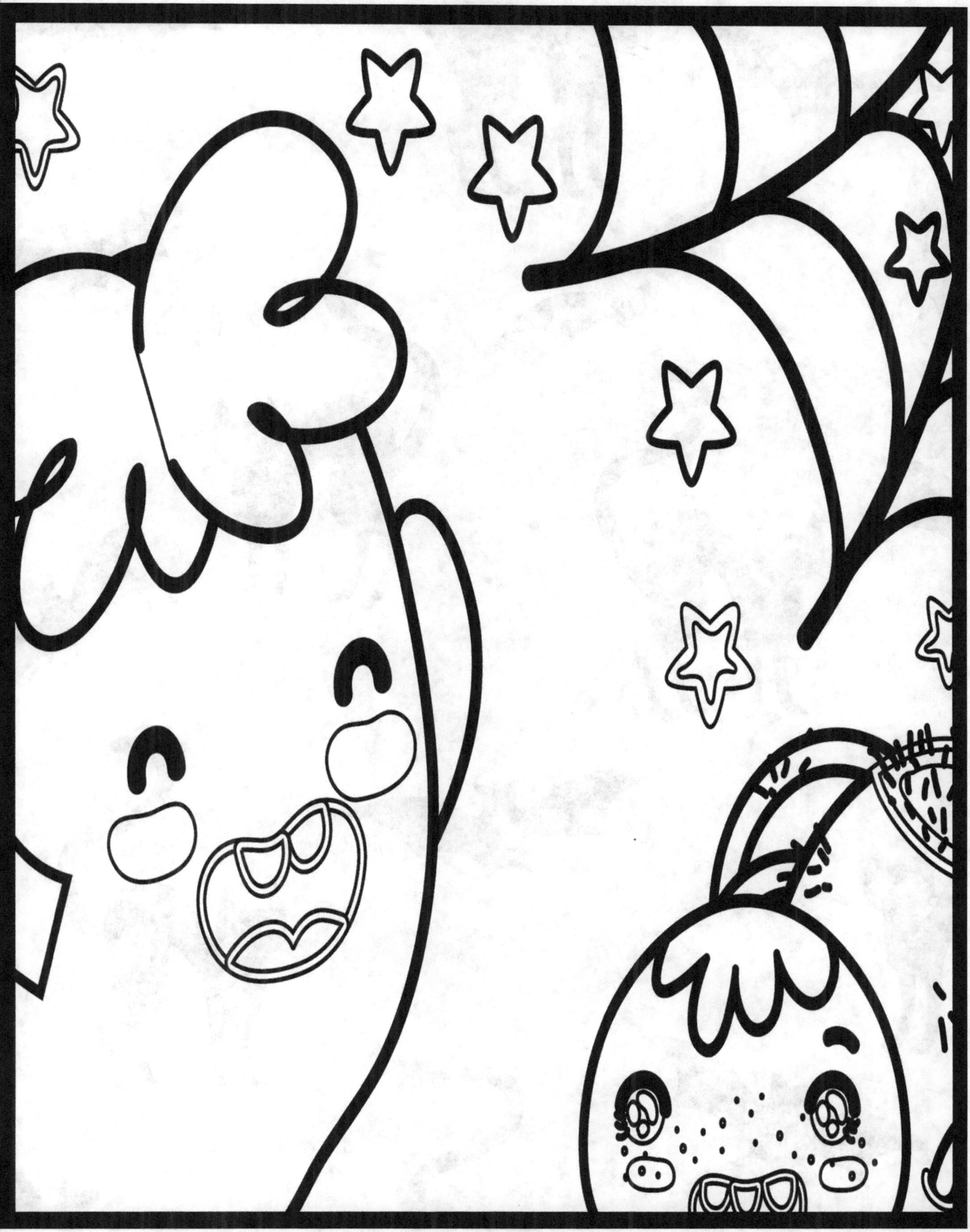

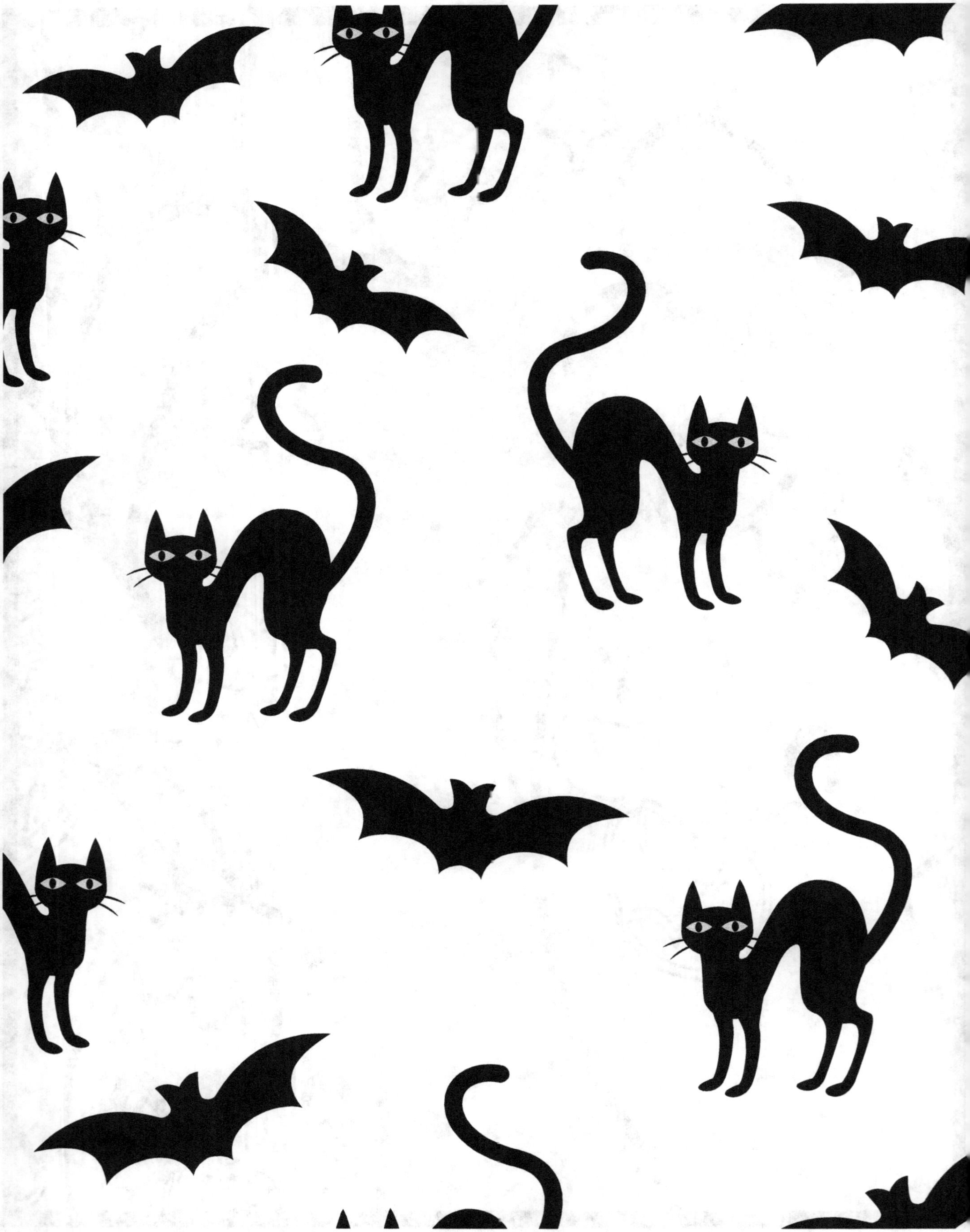

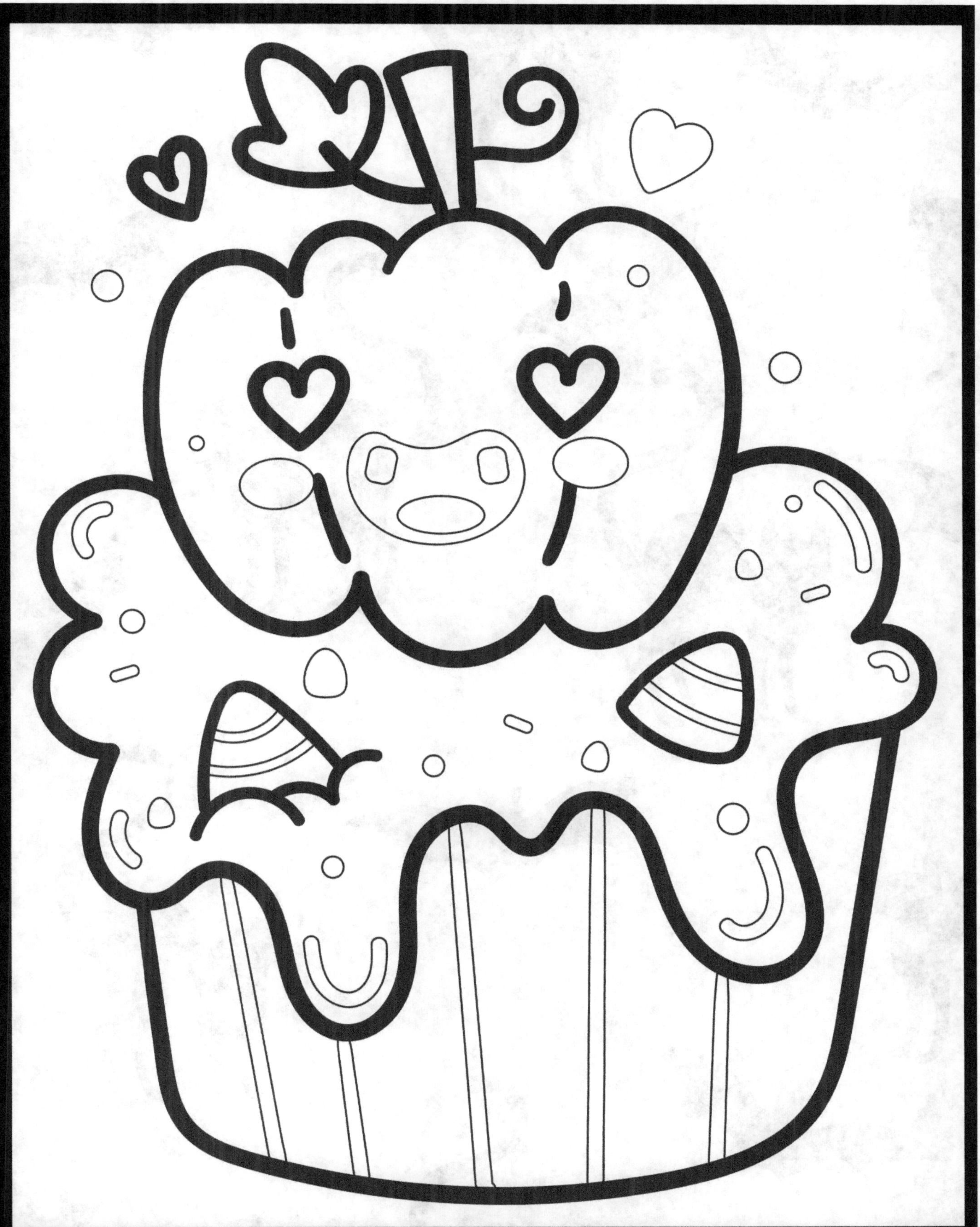

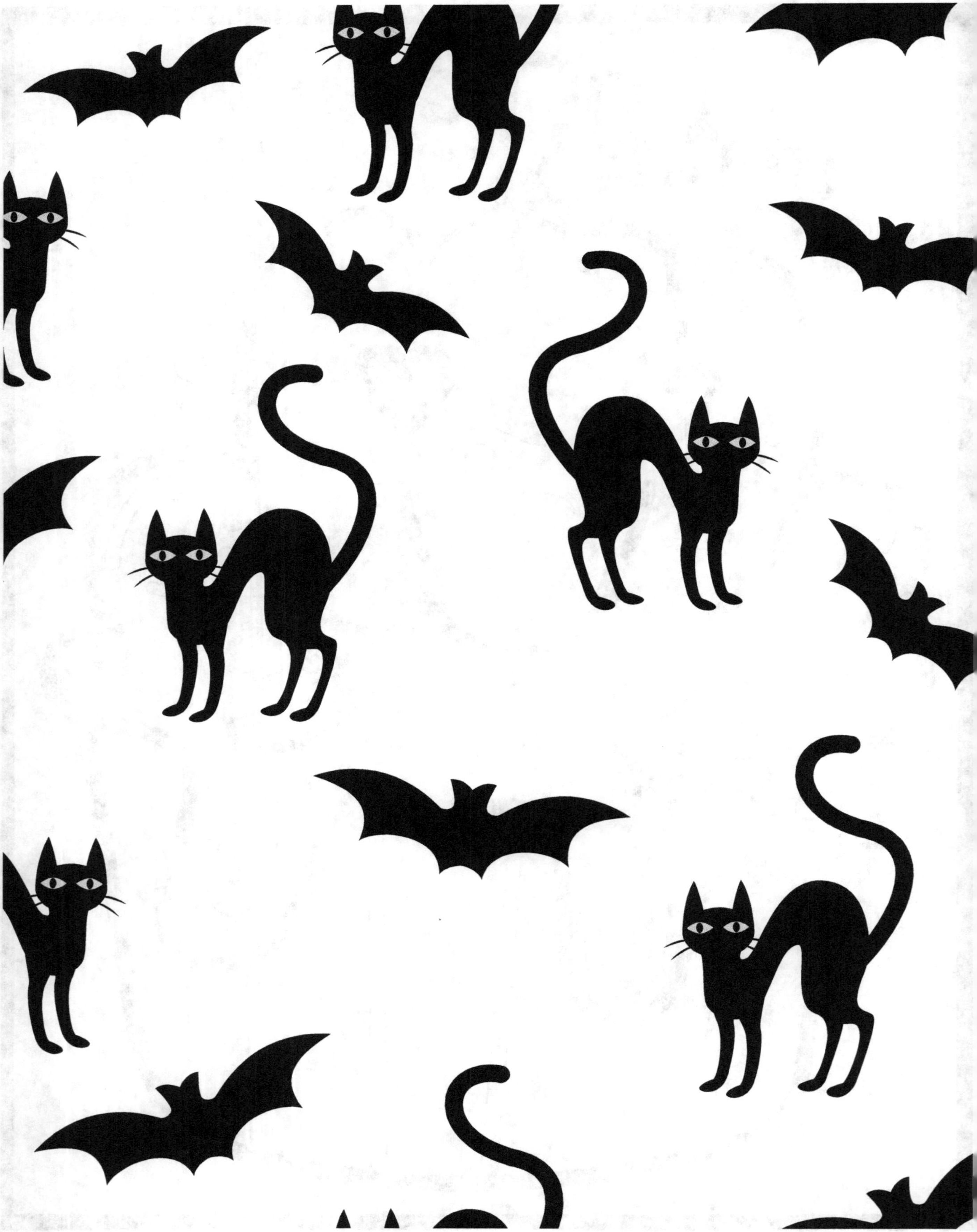

www.ingramcontent.com/pod-product-compliance
Lightning Source LLC
Chambersburg PA
CBHW081659220526
45466CB00009B/2812
* 9 7 9 8 5 5 1 6 3 5 1 4 7 *